AF840901

Richard Shuman, MD

Dr. Shuman is a first-time author. He lives with his wife, Elie, a retired nurse, in East Longmeadow, Massachusetts. They have two children: a daughter, Rachel, who is dedicated to public health work, and a son, Thomas, who is a professional actor.

BUILDING A UNICORN

Copyright © 2026 by Richard Shuman

All rights reserved. No part of this publication may be reproduced, scanned or transmitted in any form, digital or printed, without the expressed written consent of the author except in the case of brief quotations embodied in critical reviews and certain other noncommercial uses permitted by copyright.

Published by Shuman Publishing
www.richardshumanbooks.com

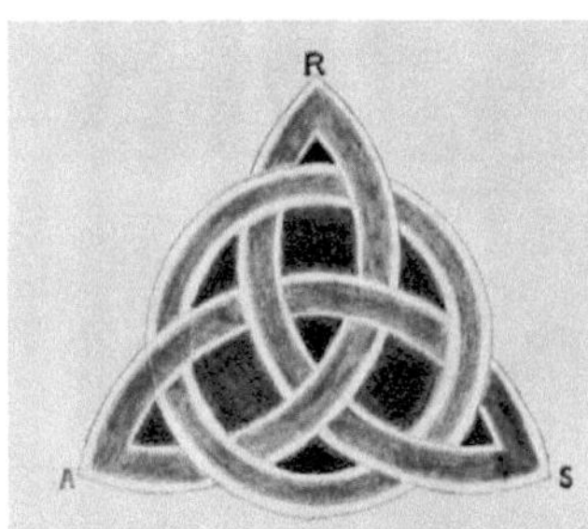

ISBN: 979-8-9959823-0-2 (paperback)

Printed in the United States of America

Cover art hand drawn by Richard Shuman, MD

Cover art inspired by Karen Stefanik MSN, RN

Praise for Dr. Richard Shuman's Building a Unicorn

"As a high school administrator for over 20 years, I found the leadership lessons in this book both relevant and applicable beyond the walls of medicine. Dr. Shuman translates complex, high-stakes experiences into clear, practical insights that resonate with anyone responsible for guiding others. This is a thoughtful, accessible guide to leadership, with insights that readily apply to my own work".

Ted McCarthy
Director Massachusetts Academy of Math & Science at WPI, Massachusetts Principal of the Year 2021

"While written by a healthcare CEO, the leadership lessons in Unicorn are truly universal. The engaging storytelling forced me to reassess my own approach with every chapter. It has inspired me to be more intentional in my interactions and to build a culture that is as productive as it is fulfilling."

Scott Donaldson, MD
Hubert E. Hatcher Family Distinguished Professor of Medicine at University of North Carolina

"Building a Unicorn" is a timely, new look at what constitutes excellent organizational culture and leadership. Dr. Shuman's unique perspective as a career physician and medical care provider brings a fresh perspective that begins with the well-being of all levels of staff, as well as clients/patients, and extends into making necessary, hard-nosed decisions that ensure organizational health. Shuman's riveting experiences and anecdotes from both the medical and management world relate, with personal humility and illumination, the bedrock of his philosophy: when the head-to-toe, whole body health of an organization is properly attended to, that organization is best-positioned to adapt to a changing world with resilience and compassion — and to have sustained success."

David J. LeLacheur, Entrepreneur

"If you want to learn more about authentic leadership and motivating your team to work hard, then this is the book for you. Rich Shuman walks you through real strategies that make people feel seen and heard. From working on the front line, to random acts of kindness, Rich's sincere approach to leadership creates both high-functioning and joyful teams that march towards the greater cause because it's the right thing to do."

Karen Stefanik, MSN, RN
Baycare Health Partners

"Building a Unicorn distills thirty years of hard-earned wisdom into stories that are at once humble, deeply human, and quietly profound. Dr. Shuman's reflections on culture, courage, and the weight of leading others will resonate with anyone navigating the realities of healthcare today. As an executive coach, I will be recommending this book often! Specific chapters are destined to become trusted guides for the leaders I walk alongside."

Kristen Woods, MD, MMM
Healthcare Executive Leadership Coach, Orcinus Health Solutions

"This wonderful book on leadership comes from a man of medicine and science. Yet it paints a vivid picture of the art of effective and ethical leadership—applicable to private, nonprofit and public sector organizations far beyond physicians and healthcare institutions. Both a life story and insightful primer on motivating excellence, it's an easy read replete with humor, humility and humanity."

Amb. (ret.) Mark P. Lagon, Ph.D.
Chief Policy Officer,
Friends of the Global Fight Against
AIDS, Tuberculosis and Malaria

Building a Unicorn: A Physician's Reflections on Organizational Culture, Leadership, and Authentic Success

To my editors Thomas Shuman and Dr Dan Weiswasser. This book would not be possible without your dedication and unwavering honesty. Thank you for helping to make this book a reality.

There are three things in life that I hold fast and prize. The first is kindness, the second is frugality and the third is humility. Be kind and you can be bold. Be frugal and you can be liberal. Be humble and you can become a leader among men.

Lao-Tse

Contents

In Memoriam: Bernice Patkin Shuman

I wish I could tell you that my mother and I had a special bond and that she inspired me to be the person I am today. I wish I could tell you that we had a great relationship and I often sought out her wisdom and guidance. I wish I could tell you that in her passing, I was able to remember only the positive aspects of our relationship. Unfortunately, none of that would be true.

The truth is that I am not entirely sure why I am mentioning her in this section. What I do know is that my mother struggled greatly both physically and emotionally throughout her life. She had a very difficult childhood and had parents who were emotionally unavailable to her. She got married at the young age of 18 and quickly had four children despite feeling quite ambivalent about having children in the first place. I was the last of her children and was certainly not planned.

My mother struggled mightily throughout her life with medical illness and, in my opinion, untreated mental illness. Despite all her challenges and all our disagreements, she always believed in me. She would routinely embellish my accomplishments with friends, family, and the local newspaper. She told me I could accomplish anything I set my mind to. She instilled in me a drive to relentlessly pursue a better version of myself. It wasn't always pretty, but she is and always will be an essential part of my life's journey.

A few years before I wrote this book, my mother passed away after a long struggle with dementia. She lived in Florida, and, at the time of her death, I was living in Connecticut. On the evening that she passed, I was sitting on my couch with my wife and felt a buzzing in my pocket. The outdoor motion sensor was alerting me to something in the front yard. Between UPS drivers delivering packages and squirrels digging in the yard, it was not unusual for the sensors to buzz all day long. I would routinely ignore these notifications and go on with my day.

However, for a reason I cannot explain, I decided to check out the notification that evening, looked out my front door, and saw four deer standing in our yard. Deer in Connecticut are not unusual, but in the several years we had been there, we had never seen one in our yard. When I opened the door, two of the deer quickly scattered, but two of them remained. I called my wife to come to the door and, by the time she got there, only one was left. It was no more than 10 to 15 yards away, staring directly at me.

I am not a religious man. After all my years in medicine, I like to think of myself as a man of science. I do not believe in reincarnation, and I am uncertain about my beliefs in life after death. I also know for certain that, just for a moment, I saw my mother in that deer. She was there to say goodbye and to let me know that she was still there and that she still believed in me.

Somewhere deep inside, I can still hear my mother telling me that I can accomplish great things and that writing a book is not a bridge too far. For that, I am forever grateful and wanted to take a moment to recognize her contribution to this book.

Dedication

I am honored to dedicate this book to my wife, Elie Shuman. About 35 years ago, I walked onto the Bone Marrow Transplant unit at Dartmouth Hitchcock Medical Center and met a brilliant and indescribably kind nurse who was caring for the sickest patients in the hospital. She had a compassion and dedication that was immediately apparent to anyone who spent more than 5 minutes with her. It took me about a month to ask her out and a couple of years to ask her to marry me, but both were the best decisions of my life.

The past three decades have been filled with significant lows and incredible highs. Our marriage is not perfect, but it is perfectly us. We have two children who are finding their way through their twenties and early thirties as Elie and I embark on the third act of our life's journey. It is a time when we will start to think about our legacy, life's meaning, and, hopefully, grandchildren. We will need to find a new path to grow both independently and together. I know we will find those answers together.

I often look at other couples and hear of their great travel adventures or watch their amazing accomplishments on Instagram. Elie and I don't travel much, and we don't post a lot. Our lives are much quieter than that. We have instead found tremendous joy in the small aspects of life: a lovely gluten-free meal, a TV show that makes us laugh, a walk with our golden retriever (Molly), or new plants for our garden. It is in these small, quiet moments that I realize that I have found a life partner. It is to this incredible person that I dedicate this book.

Introduction

My longtime friend Dr. Dan Weiswasser and I were having breakfast overlooking the Pioneer Valley in Western Massachusetts. It was a beautiful spring morning, and we were catching up on our personal lives and professional challenges. I told Dan that I was considering becoming an executive coach after my current role, but I was a little anxious about making a career change as I approached the age of 60. He looked at me and said, "You would be a great executive coach. In fact, you should write a book about being a physician leader." I laughed off the compliment and finished eating my omelet.

Several days later, when I was experiencing an existential crisis about the "third act" of my life, I revisited that conversation. Did I have something to say? Would people, other than my immediate family and friends, be interested in hearing my thoughts? Do people still read books? Most concerning of all, was I a good enough writer to put my thoughts into a coherent and compelling book? Given the uncertainty presented by all these questions, I decided to put the idea on the pile of things I would get to when I had time, something I would consider in retirement.

Several weeks later, I visited my son, Thomas, in New York. I know everyone says this about their kids, but I have a truly brilliant son. He is one of the smartest people I know and is pursuing a career in acting. When he was at Georgetown, he double majored in Political Science and Theater and minored in Arabic. However, what has always been most compelling about Thomas is his insatiable desire to learn. He is a voracious reader who takes tremendous pride in his NYC library card and is so incredibly well read that he was the perfect choice to edit this book (Editor's Note: Thanks, Dad!). When I mentioned the idea of writing a book about being a physician leader to him, he was incredibly supportive, and his support inspired me to move this project from the "Do It Later" pile to the "Do It Now" pile. Several weeks after our discussion, he sent me a writing pad, pencils, and a waterproof idea board for the shower (where I typically get my best ideas). His kindness and support touched my heart. He later texted, noting that I had always supported him and now it was his turn to return the favor.

I would love to say that writing a book was on my bucket list or even on my top 30 list of "Things That Bring Me Joy". Truthfully, it didn't make it onto either. After 30 years of being a physician and a leader, I feel compelled to share stories and insights that, had I known them earlier, would have made me a more effective leader and helped my organizations thrive.

This book centers on storytelling with occasional leadership insights. There is no magic and no "secret formula" for success. Many of the concepts shared here are not new, but, in the context of lived experience, they may resonate with you. A mentor told me that once you find three interesting facts in a leadership book, you can stop reading and move on to the next book. Although I would feel great if you read this entire book, I would also be thrilled if you found three concepts that resonated with you.

My editor told me this is the part where I'm supposed to introduce myself. I guess this could be in a separate "About the author" section, but those always seemed a little pretentious to me. I would rather just try to slip this part in, under the radar and late in the introduction.

I grew up in the Boston suburbs. I am the youngest of four children, with two brothers and one sister. I love Boston sports teams and through my life have been an avid golfer. As you can tell from the title of the book, I am a physician but, to be honest, I never wanted to be a doctor. As an undergraduate at Harvard, I concentrated on 17th-century Dutch art, particularly the masterworks of Rembrandt and Vermeer. It turns out, however, that a career in art history is quite challenging, so I decided to pursue a path that would provide me with a more stable and predictable life. I have never given up my passion for art, and it remains a part of my life to this day. I even took the leap of faith to do the unicorn illustration on the cover of this book.

I had the privilege of attending the University of Massachusetts Medical School and then completing my Internal Medicine Residency at Dartmouth Hitchcock Medical Center. After completing my training, and meeting my future wife, we moved to Western Massachusetts to be closer to family. I never thought that we would stay in this part of the state when we moved here over 3 decades ago, but the area has a special charm and seems likely to be our forever home.

In Western Massachusetts, I worked as an Internal Medicine physician for over two decades at RiverBend Medical Group. During my tenure at RiverBend, I gradually progressed through the ranks, serving as Assistant Chief of Medicine, Chief of Medicine, Medical Director, and ultimately as CEO. Trinity Health ultimately acquired the company. As part of the transition, I became the President of the Trinity Health Of New England Medical Group before taking a job in 2019 as the CEO of Baycare Health Partners, an organization focused on population health. In mid 2025, with the support of my wife, I made the decision to retire and pursue the long list of items on my "things that bring me joy" list.

This book is titled "Building a Unicorn", based on an idea I borrowed from my close nurse friend Karen Stefanik. She would routinely share with me that the organizational culture that existed within our company was so special and rare that it was like a unicorn. To this day, whenever we see a picture of this magical creature, we text it to each other. The primary focus of this book is to share with the reader the key steps to creating an amazing organizational culture. The book definitely has a medical bent but is targeted at anyone who is a leader or aspires to become one. Hopefully, by the end of this book, you will have some meaningful insights into how to build your own unicorn.

1

Building an Organizational Culture

"The only thing of real importance that leaders do is to create and manage culture and that the unique talent of leaders is their ability to work with a culture."

Professor Edgar Schein

It is a dilemma faced by every organizational leader. How do you create the right culture? A discussion of mission, vision, and values usually follows. Judging by these discussions, all you need are some Foundational Structures, Organizational Pillars, Compass Points, and a nice PowerPoint, and there you have it - the building blocks for a great company culture.

I wish it were that easy. The number of hours that highly paid, intelligent leaders spend on wordsmithing every aspect of their mission, vision, and supporting documents is unbelievable. If that wasn't enough, leaders frequently bring in consultants to help guide them through the process. There are times that you need subject matter experts from outside your organization but that should be the exception, not the rule. Your leaders know more about your organization than anyone else ever will. It is essential to trust them with the big decisions and let them define, create, and instill your culture. I have found that the best way to define your culture is to focus on your organizational values. If you can define the values of your organization, then you have essentially defined your culture. I would like to pause here and offer you both a warning and a caveat.

My warning is that, as a leader, you must invest a significant amount of time and thought into defining your values and then honestly commit to living them. It is easy to espouse values but putting them into clear and consistent practice is what distinguishes good from great leadership. Living your values as a leader is not sufficient to create the culture you want, but failing to live them will certainly destroy it.

My caveat is that if you sit in a room with only other leaders and try to set the values of your organization, these values will never fully resonate with your employees. It is essential to set organizational values as a whole organization, not just as a senior leadership team. The problem with developing culture through complex structures, charts, and consultant slide decks is that nobody remembers it once the meeting ends. Documents typically sit on a web page or on a piece of paper that nobody looks at. In fact, even the senior leaders who created these documents may struggle to articulate their views on them.

This is the dilemma that most senior leaders experience. There is a desire to provide a comprehensive vision and thorough documentation that conveys to the rest of the world how thoughtful they are. Unfortunately, this creates a significant gap between theory and practice. This problem is not limited to the development of culture; it can also be observed in discussions of organizational goals. Most organizations have numerous concurrent goals that prevent them from focusing their resources and employees on the priorities that will drive growth and sustain their business.

It is with this in mind that I encourage leaders to look first at their organizational values. In most companies, this typically consists of a list of 5 to 7 items. I am sure that they are all important, but I would ask that you consider choosing one value and making this the focus of your organizational culture.

I can see you rolling your eyes. You are barely through the first chapter of this book, and this pretentious doctor is telling you to set aside 95% of the documentation your senior leadership team has developed in the past 6 months. I realize prioritization is incredibly difficult, especially in complex organizations. Every value is important, every organizational pillar is important, and every clinical guideline is important; all these things deserve our attention. Unfortunately, when we cannot crystallize priorities as leaders, we fail to become truly effective leaders. Prioritization and exclusion are not the same thing. You can prioritize certain items while still addressing others.

Let's try an example. In my last organization, the following values were created by the employees:

1. ***Compassion***: We intentionally perform acts of kindness
2. ***Teamwork***: We speak with and for, not against each other
3. ***Leadership***: We act with integrity and humility
4. ***Personal Integrity***: We advocate for others as if they were our family
5. ***Accountability***: We own our decisions and our work

I was very proud of this organization in no small part because of these values. The organization was far from perfect, but the employees were truly dedicated to their patients and had a commitment to one key principle that overlaid all the others: they strove to consistently to "Do the Right Thing". Not the easy thing, not the fun thing, not the financially beneficial thing, but the "Right Thing". Although not explicitly stated in the guiding principles, it was a core value that defined the culture. When you asked people in the organization if they knew the five values, they likely would not know them verbatim, but they all knew that the organization constantly strove to do the "right thing". Imagine having an organization where everyone knew the culture's one core principle and truly believed in it. Imagine its impact on morale, recruitment, and retention. Even if complete permeation was a long shot, the changes you would see in striving for this goal would blow you away.

So how do you make this happen? I must admit to being frustrated with leaders who have great ideas but lack a clear understanding of how to operationalize them. Similarly, consultants routinely annoy me because they so rarely understand an organization well enough to provide meaningful operational advice.

Creating cultural change is a slow, painful, and difficult process. As one of my colleagues eloquently put it, "it's a f***ing slog!" In a society seeking quick answers to complex problems, organizational cultural change requires slow, methodical introspection and implementation. This book isn't full of quick fixes and, in my humble yet experienced opinion, any book that suggests them won't work.

The first key to cultural change is you. If you are the leader of an organization, you must commit yourself to its core organizational values. If you are not willing to do this, then the rest of this book is simply a waste of time. I know what you're thinking: "Of course I'm willing to commit. I want to do the Right Thing." Ok, take a deep breath and think about this example:

You are a physician leader in a multispecialty group with two surgeons. They both generate a significant amount of revenue, which helps keep the lights on. Recruiting surgeons to your area is extremely difficult. One of the surgeons exhibits behaviors that are not consistent with your guiding principles. The surgeon yells at nurses in the hallways, demeans the secretaries in the waiting room and routinely uses foul language. Despite multiple interventions, their behavior continues to be problematic. You are left with two choices:

1. Fire the surgeon. This aligns with your values, but it puts the organization at significant financial risk. This decision could also result in losing the other surgeon because they do not want to do the additional work to cover the loss of this key clinical contributor.
2. Continue to employ the surgeon and sideline your organizational values.

Being a leader doesn't seem like so much fun anymore, does it? If you are genuinely committed to living your organizational values, you would fire the surgeon. The impact of a decision like this is monumental when setting the culture. Firing the problematic surgeon will signal to your staff that no one is above the organizational values, will empower the nurses and the receptionists to report individuals who use their positional authority to demean others, and, perhaps most importantly, will create a safe environment where people feel valued and respected.

Sometimes leaders do not realize how much they are being watched. Your employees are constantly looking to see if a leader is exemplifying the organization's values. It may seem unfair that you are experiencing so much scrutiny, but it is the reality of leadership. Employees will notice your clothes, your grooming, your eating habits, your sense of humor, and who you eat lunch with. All these behaviors influence how people perceive you, but nothing is as important as living the values of your organization.

As a senior leader, I was present at a meeting where the hospital's CEO was tasked with making a difficult decision. The hospital was involved in a contract that put the system at financial risk for providing care for Medicaid patients. The details of the arrangement are not important but suffice it to say the hospital system was losing millions of dollars. Some senior leaders suggested that this approach was not financially viable and that we should abandon this strategy.

I will never forget the moment when the CEO of the hospital decided to do the right thing over the financially expedient one. He looked at people in the room and said, "We will not abandon our mission to serve the poor and underserved. We will absorb this financial loss and continue to find ways to make this strategy successful". At the time, many leaders questioned his decision. Several years later, the contract was shown to be financially successful and of tremendous benefit to the community.

These are just two examples that highlight why it's essential for leaders to embody the values of the organization. There are so many more that occur every day, every week, and across a career. The commitment must be sustained if you are going to build a great culture and a truly successful organization. Culture can't be built by just one person living the organization's values. To this end, the next chapter will explore the concept of the "bottom 15%" and its impact on organizational culture.

2

The Bottom 15%

"When you make a decision, however large or small, do not ask "what is the easy thing to do" or "what will cost the least money?" or "what will make me the most loved or popular by those affected by the decision?" Just ask what the right decision is, all things considered. Once you have made that judgment, and you will make it better once you have been burned a few times, then just do it, decide it, no matter how difficult it is, no matter how costly, no matter how unpopular. In the long run, whatever the immediate uproar or inconveniences, people, your people, will respect you for following your conscience, for doing what you thought right, even though they do not agree with you."

Reverend John Cavanaugh
Former President Univ. Notre Dame

Every organizational leader experiences the same challenge: "How should I handle my poorest performers?" The idea that roughly 15% of an organization may fall into the "low performer" group is not new. These individuals can have a massive impact on your organization, and failing to address this properly will stall the adoption of your organizational culture. Consider this anecdote: When walking back to my office in the medical center, I rounded the corner and heard the quiet but distinct sound of a woman crying. As I looked up from the papers in my hand, I saw that the woman was a receptionist. She'd been with the organization for a long time and was a valuable part of our front-line team. She was stifling tears as she continued to check in patients. I approached her and asked if she was ok. She responded, a little startled by unexpectedly seeing the CEO, that she was fine. It was very clear that she was, in fact, not fine, but it was also clear by the tone of her voice that she did not want to discuss the situation. I decided to leave the waiting room but, as I was departing, a physician who worked in that area approached the receptionist and began to yell at her. He was quite loud and used very colorful language. Every patient in the waiting room could hear the interaction. I reentered the reception desk area and asked the physician to join me in a quiet area of the office.

After sitting the physician down in a quiet room, I asked him to share his story. He noted that he was pretty upset with the receptionist because she was taking too much time checking people in, which was making him run late. He noted this wasn't the first occurrence and expressed his desire for her to be disciplined. As he continued sharing the story, his anger grew, and his voice began to rise. I gave him all the time he needed to share his thoughts and tried very hard not to interrupt, using nonverbal cues to prompt him to continue. Eventually, he finished his thoughts.

I wish I could say that over the 30 years of working with healthcare providers, this was a unique interaction, but that would not be truthful. I certainly wanted to believe that professionals who entered a field focused on helping others would maintain a higher standard of personal interactions. Unfortunately, that is not the case. It appears that people are people, and there is always a "bottom 15%". Having a medical degree does not exclude you from bad behavior, but it has been my experience that sometimes it insulates you from the repercussions of your behavior.

It was at this point that I utilized an elementary but important leadership tool: the AID feedback model. The AID model is an acronym that stands for "Action", "Impacts", and "Desired Outcome". Simply put, your goal is to share the details of a specific Action, discuss the Impacts of that Action and, finally, review the Desired Outcome as a next step. It is not something that I have developed, but I have found it to be helpful in dealing with challenging situations as well as in building culture. I want to point out that there are many feedback models. I have chosen the AID model because I like its simplicity and focus on impact. You should choose the one that fits your style and use it consistently both for negative and positive feedback.

In the case of this physician, I started by acknowledging his concerns. He was clearly upset, and it is always a reasonable first step to reinforce that you are a good listener and have heard what is being said. I followed that by talking about the "Action" under concern: he had yelled at a receptionist in a public space. He had used his positional authority to demean another person. After sharing this with him, I spent a good deal of time talking about the "Impact" of his "Action". He created a hostile work environment. He violated the organization's values and negatively impacted its reputation. In addition, he injured the culture by suggesting that the organizational values and expectations don't apply to physicians.

After we finished that part of the conversation, I asked him, "What do you think we should do next?". He replied, "I think you should send the receptionist for training and remove her from my area until she can work faster". As you might imagine, this was not the answer I was looking for; I had hoped for a response that demonstrated humility and self-awareness. I often must remind myself that if the individual possessed those qualities, we would not be having this discussion in the first place. I took an internal deep breath and redirected the response.

I acknowledged the potential need for additional training but brought the issue back to the physician and guided him to the "Desired Outcome" that he needed to apologize to the receptionist. He reluctantly agreed and publicly apologized. Later that week, I met with this physician again and provided him with written discipline.

Three months later, he repeated his inappropriate behavior by yelling at a nurse in the hallway, and he was released from the organization. At the time of the initial incident, I was very happy that I was able to intervene, use the AID model, and convince the physician to apologize. I was focused on how this physician behaved and the process that was required to document this painful interaction. What I did not fully appreciate was the impact that this interaction would have on the organizational culture.

Several days after the interaction with this physician, the receptionist showed up at my office door and asked to speak with me. She shared with me that she was relatively new to our organization but had worked in healthcare for a long time. She had frequently noted how physicians were treated differently from the rest of the staff. Somehow, it was deemed acceptable for physicians to use their positional authority to demean others without consequences. She then said something that I will never forget: "This is the first time I have seen a leader treat everyone by the same set of rules. I am proud to work here, and I have told all my colleagues and friends what you did."

It is easy to think of this as a single act by an organizational leader. However, I would ask you to think about this in a different context. When, as a leader, you interact with the "Bottom 15%" and allow their behaviors to persist, you are destroying your culture. You are choosing not to live by your values, and your inaction is very noticeable to everyone. In contrast, when you visibly live your values, you quickly build a strong culture.

In my years as a leader, I've found that the inability to address the bottom 15% is a defining barrier to success. It takes courage and training to work with challenging individuals, and most organizations prefer to avoid these issues. By avoiding the challenge, they undermine their culture and limit their future success.

People often ask me, "How do I identify the bottom 15%?". The truth is that this identification can be significantly impacted by unconscious bias. Many tools evaluate how individuals perform in their job, but this is not always reflective of how someone fits with the values and culture of the organization. In many organizations, physicians are not evaluated by the staff. Their reviews focus on the volume of patients seen, revenue production, and performance on quality metrics. Humility, collaboration, and emotional intelligence are often overlooked. In addition, these key factors that build a culture are often overlooked in the hiring and retention of physicians. The other major confounder arises when leaders build an organization in their own image. People who do not conform to their view of the world and sense of diversity and inclusion are often considered problematic and potentially inappropriately placed in the bottom 15%.

There is no clear answer to identifying those who don't meet the organizational culture. However, in this specific case, I would not minimize your subjective feelings. It should not be your only criterion but permit yourself to allow subjectivity to be part of your overall assessment.

Finally, once you have identified your bottom 15%, make sure to have a meaningful process to provide these individuals with the tools and resources they need to be successful in your organization and move to the "Middle 70%". The key to your organizational success will be how much time and how many resources you provide to this challenging segment of your organization versus everyone else. We will discuss this important concept and employee retention in the next section.

3

The Middle 70%

"It is the emotional involvement of people deep within an organization that is essential to cultural change."

Thomas Horton

70% is admittedly an arbitrary number, but it is the concept that matters. When you look at your organization, you can likely divide it into three groups: Early Adopters, Resistors, and The Middle. The concept of employee cohorts within organizations isn't new, but how you engage these groups to shape culture is the focus of this chapter.

In 2005, my organization decided to adopt an electronic medical record (EMR). The idea of an EMR was relatively novel at the time; most physicians had only ever known a paper medical chart. Furthermore, the transition was expected to be extremely expensive and would result in a significant change to the group's workflows.

A project team of physicians and staff were created to prepare the organization for the transition. The EMR company suggested that the project would take a year, but we felt we could accomplish this transition in 6 months. We really had no idea what we were committing to at the time.

The process of moving from a paper record to an electronic record was a daunting task. Most people think that the abstraction of data (manual movement of data from the paper record to the electronic record) is the most challenging aspect of this transition. Although that aspect is very time-consuming, it is the transition to new workflows and the development of group preferences that turned out to be the most culturally difficult. I will never forget sitting in a pizza shop with my friend Dr. Dan Weiswasser, reviewing the Physicians' Desk Reference one page at a time. For those unfamiliar with this reference book, it lists all the prescription medications available at that time. It seems almost unbelievable, given the state of technology today, that this information was not easily accessible electronically, but that's how it was at the time. Dan and I sat for hours going through every page of that book, picking out the most common medications and dosages to customize preferences in the EMR. We spent equally endless hours developing documentation templates and order sets.

By the time 6 months had come and gone, we were ready to go live. Unfortunately, what we had not adequately prepared for was how the providers and staff would accept the transition. We believed we were prepared, but our focus on the mechanics of the transition left us unready for the cultural change that followed.

The individuals on the transition team were invested entirely in the process. There was excitement and a feeling that we were fulfilling a greater purpose, that our work had great meaning, and that we were positively impacting the lives of our patients. We were the "early adopters" or the "top 15%". Interestingly, since the process so engaged us, we had an underlying feeling that everyone else would feel similarly. We were wrong.

On October 31, 2005, I sat in a large conference room with several other members of the transition team as our medical group turned on the electronic medical record. At first, it was quiet, and there was a sense that we would have a smooth transition. Then the phone rang - there was an issue with checking in a patient. This was followed by a call from a physician having trouble placing a medical order and then from a physician assistant having challenges with documentation. Over the next 8 hours, we filled the poster boards on the walls of the conference room with concerns and complaints. It was overwhelming and disheartening.

An outstanding, well-respected physician came to see me and broke down in tears because she felt so overwhelmed by this transition. As the physician leader of the transition team, I thought that I had failed the organization. In retrospect, I realized that, although the go-live for the EMR was an important day, what happened over the next six months would ultimately determine the success and define the culture of the organization.

The transition team spent every day over the next several weeks addressing issues from the go-live, as well as tracking and resolving new ones. Certain physicians were very vocal about their concerns and demanded additional resources. They also threatened to leave the group if things did not improve quickly. They frequently shared their issues with the rest of the staff and reminisced about the "good old days" of paper charts.

The transition team focused its efforts on the people who complained the most. Since we had limited resources, this meant we struggled to support everyone. The squeaky wheels got the grease, and the bottom 15% garnered over 50% of the transition team's attention. At the time, I did not notice or care about the implications of our support decisions. We just wanted to make the system functional and effectuate a transition that allowed us to see patients.

It wasn't until a year later, when we started to perform provider satisfaction surveys, that the actual impact of our leadership decisions became clear. The providers who had complained the most and received the most support, resources, and attention still did not like the electronic medical record. The providers on the transition team, who were more technically focused, loved the new system. Everyone else felt somewhere in between. The problem was that the "everyone else" category made up over 60% of the respondents.

When we began conducting small-group provider optimization training, the issue became even clearer. The resistors, despite receiving additional support and training, were barely getting by and showed no interest in optimizing their workflows. They continued to yearn for the paper record. The early adopters had embraced the transition and had optimized their use of the EMR.

What shocked us most, however, was "everyone else". These individuals had learned enough to get through their day but had not embraced the EMR. They were inefficient and had never reached out to get the resources they needed to improve their use of the EMR. They had suffered in silence.

In retrospect, it becomes easier to see the leadership mistake I had made. The transition team had utilized over 50% of its resources on the bottom 15%. Additionally, it allocated a significant portion of its remaining resources to the early adopters. This left very little time for the Middle 70%.

<u>This is one of the most critical and difficult leadership lessons in this book</u>. Great organizations apply almost all their organizational resources to the Middle 70%. You need to provide the Bottom 15% with reasonable resources since some of them may choose to join the Middle 70%. By the same token, you need to enable the early adopters to continue to innovate. However, your focus needs to be on the Middle 70% to allow them to move upwards towards the Top 15%.

It sounds so easy when you put it into just a few sentences. I promise you that it is tough. It is hard to disregard the people who complain the loudest. It is equally challenging to spend less time with the early adopters since they often share a vision with you and are fun to hang out with. Convincing people in the middle to follow the organization's vision and direction is one of the most critical factors in building a significant and sustainable culture.

4

Hiring to Build Culture

"You're only as good as the people you hire."

Ray Kroc

The most common question I get when talking about culture is "How long will it take to build the culture we want?" The standard answer is that it depends on the organization, the leadership, the commitment to change, and the organizational resources. Although this is a perfectly reasonable answer, I find it completely unsatisfactory.

When I have had the opportunity to work with consultants, the typical answer I have heard is that building a culture takes two to three years. I believe this is the answer because people generally prefer not to hear that it might take longer. There is a level of impatience that is evident in healthcare, and perhaps society, that is uncomfortable with delayed satisfaction and long-term goals. Because this entire book focuses on the key steps to building a culture, you can begin to grasp the time and effort required to make this monumental change.

I am not a big fan of cliffhangers, so here is the answer: cultural change takes at least 6 years. (This is where you dog-ear the page since it represents a key takeaway.) I know that this is not a popular answer, and many leaders share remarkable stories of quick transformations. The truth, however, is that to build a great culture, it must permeate the entire organization, and that takes time. Three key things must happen:

1. Dismissal of a significant portion of the Bottom 15% (we will talk about this more in the next chapter).
2. Engagement of the Middle 70% (this was the previous chapter)
3. Recruitment of people into your organization who embody and enhance the culture that you seek (we are going to talk about this now)

Over the years, I have hired hundreds of employees. When I first started to interview candidates, I would ask the standard interview questions, such as:

1. Tell me about yourself?
2. Why are you changing jobs?
3. What experience makes you qualified for this job?
4. Tell me about how you handle stressful situations?

I am sure that I posed a bunch of other uninspired questions that I choose not to recall at this time. These interview questions provided me with minimal information and even less information that was meaningful. I would often make decisions based on a gut feeling or, worse, unconscious bias. My hiring success rate was average, and to be honest, the idea of hiring to build a culture never crossed my mind. I was just happy that we found someone with a pulse who could help us manage a large cohort of patients.

During one of my sessions with my executive coach, Gina Ohanesian, MSOB (a concept I later dedicate an entire chapter of this book to), we found ourselves discussing the interview and hiring process. She asked a question that I still think about today: "What are you looking for when you are hiring individuals for your organization?" Gina never accepted a simple answer like, "Someone who has a pulse", so I was forced to think about this answer carefully. It was at that point she introduced me to the work of Patrick Lencioni.

If you have not had the opportunity to read Lencioni's writing, I would highly recommend it. I am not going to go into significant detail because you should read his work yourself, but I am going to highlight one key concept. Lencioni recommends that, when you are hiring, you consider three key factors: humility, work ethic, and emotional intelligence. This concept really resonated with me. The idea of hiring people who are humble, hardworking, and emotionally intelligent would really allow me to build the culture I was looking for. Lencioni went on to develop interview questions that assessed these characteristics. These are available online if you are interested (and you should be).

Whether all the characteristics should be weighed equally is a decision you should make based on the culture you are looking to build. However, in my opinion, humility is by far the most crucial characteristic to consider when hiring for culture. I have found that someone who can acknowledge the accomplishments of others without seeking the spotlight is exactly the right leader around whom to build a culture.

Over time, I have added a fourth hiring characteristic: joy. This assessment is subjective, but it's usually clear whether an interviewee adds energy and positivity to the conversation. Many jobs involve a degree of repetition, which can foster a sense of heaviness and mental fatigue. It takes a joyful person to bring purpose to their work and energy to the workplace.

In my last work environment before retiring, I had two colleagues named Kathy and Karen. They were the most joyful leaders I had ever worked with. I was not the one who hired them, but I wished I had been. They were humble, hardworking, emotionally intelligent, and incredibly joyful. Kathy's laugh was amazing and raised the spirits of everyone around her. Karen's smile and positive energy lifted the spirits of everyone in the office and anyone she talked to. No matter what their day was like, they always found time to smile and bring joy to the workplace. Their joy was a defining feature of the organizational culture.

This all brings me back to the question of why it takes six years to build culture. The simple answer is that it takes a long time to hire enough people who fit your culture and let go enough people who don't to reach a meaningful tipping point. If you do this too fast, you create instability, which can limit your ability to create culture. If you go too slow, you may lose your way and not be able to retain the new hires who have joined your organization because it promises a meaningful culture. I have found that 6 years is the sweet spot.

If all you had to do were hire the right people, the job of building a culture would be fun and relatively easy. Unfortunately, addressing the resistors is essential to creating a great culture. In the next chapter, we will take on this daunting but essential task.

5

Time to Let Go

"The day firing becomes easy is the day to fire yourself."

Tom Peters

It was a warm, sunny day, and I was eating a late breakfast with my long-time friend, Shelley Jackson. At the time, she was the head of a school in Deerfield, Massachusetts. We were talking about the challenges of leading an organization when I asked her something I was always curious about: "How do you emotionally handle firing a staff member?" I really wanted to understand how someone I truly admired handled the daunting task of letting someone go.

This was clearly something Shelley had thought about before. She hesitated before admitting that parting ways with staff is, without question, the most challenging aspect of her role. That surprised me a little since, as a head of school, she had to deal with teenage children and their parents. I asked her why it was so challenging. She noted that it required a lot of emotional energy and that she had previously worried about creating a significant hardship for that individual.

Shelley paused again and then provided me with advice that I carry around with me to this day. She said, "Although it is still hard to fire people, I look at it differently now. The truth is that most of these individuals are not happy in their current situation. They are not thriving in their roles and, consequently, often create situations that require correction. By letting them go, I am giving them a new opportunity to find happiness and joy in a new role and a new environment. I don't expect them to ever thank me, but I know I am doing the right thing not only for the organization but for them as well."

I immediately realized that this conversation would make me a better leader. I also knew that I had to spend some more time reflecting on my own challenges with respect to firing people. I began to coalesce around a realization: physicians are not necessarily great organizational leaders.

Spend a moment and think about why many individuals become physicians. The most common answer is that they want to help people. You also hear that they are intelligent and passionate about science and technology. You are rarely told that they went into medicine to become organizational leaders. I have occasionally joked that the initials "MD" have many meanings for me. These have included "my dad", "medical director", "medical doctor", and "major dufus", and, at different times in my life, I have embraced each of these roles. It is interesting how many people assume that physicians possess broad intelligence, as if having the title of "MD" makes you a savvy businessperson or a natural leader.

The path to becoming a physician is long and arduous and is not the focus of this book. However, it is essential to have a basic understanding of this path to better comprehend why many physicians may struggle with becoming successful leaders. Interestingly, these same reasons apply to many others trying to lead an organization.

The path to medical school often begins in high school, focusing on those with an interest and ability in science. If you also demonstrate decent interpersonal skills and a desire to help others, the decision to become a physician becomes compelling.

As you enter the pre-med track in college, you are immediately immersed in the most challenging science courses, taking physics, inorganic chemistry, and organic chemistry courses in your first year. These are intended to weed out people who are not dedicated or smart enough to be doctors. Unfortunately, these courses often instead weed out intelligent individuals who might grow into exceptional physicians but struggle to grasp the molecular structure of a peanut.

The pain and agony continue as you are forced to complete a grueling scientific curriculum, bereft of a proper liberal arts education. Don't let the colleges fool you when they say that the pre-med track offers a well-rounded curriculum. In most cases, you are required to take a few entry-level classes in other subjects, but most of your classes are predetermined by the need to meet your premed requirements.

As you finish up your college career, you are required to take the MCATs, which are basically the medical school equivalent of the SATs. If you are lucky and talented enough to survive the college gauntlet and perform well on standardized testing, you take the next step on the medical journey: medical school. I loved medical school, but for many, the endless hours of studying in isolation can be overwhelming. The typical medical school experience consists of two years of studying followed by two years of clinical rotations. You are so busy that most of your medical school social experience is defined by the other students in your school.

By the end of medical school, if you have not taken any breaks in your educational journey, you are typically twenty-six years old and entering your internship and residency. You are indeed a doctor, but you are still in training. The following three years (and potentially more, depending on your specialty) are physically and emotionally grueling. Your entire life revolves around other residents who are experiencing the same journey as you. You spend your waking hours (and the few that can be spent sleeping) in the hospital. Although the residency experience has improved a bit since my training the basic tenets remain the same. You are there to learn your craft through a long and intense hands-on apprenticeship.

After you emerge from your residency, you continue your training in a subspecialty, or you start your clinical practice. I have often said that becoming a physician involves giving up your twenties so you can enjoy your sixties. Although this is an exaggeration, there is no doubt that you make a significant personal sacrifice to become a physician. In addition, the training is highly focused on preparing you to become a clinician.

I think it is essential to repeat the thought in my last sentence: the training to become a physician prepares you to be a competent clinician. You spend thousands of hours developing the tools to manage patients and accumulating the scientific knowledge to solve clinical problems. The training, however, does not significantly focus on your interpersonal skills or the skills needed to be a strong organizational leader.

In fact, I would argue that individuals who become physicians lack many of the qualities you would look for in an organizational leader. In my experience, physicians are often very compassionate but struggle with conflict. They enjoy one-on-one interactions but avoid group dynamics. They find solace in scientific knowledge but struggle with uncertainty. Perhaps most concerning, many physicians struggle with interpersonal skills and emotional intelligence—qualities that are essential for effective organizational leadership.

It is not my intention to denigrate physicians; I am genuinely proud of the profession and the individuals who serve in the medical field. I want to show, however, how the selection process and arduous training for physicians might result in professionals who may not always be the best suited to become organizational leaders. Indeed, the idea that if you are a good doctor, you will be a good leader is not accurate.

As I left my meeting with Shelley, I began to question my own leadership abilities. Upon reflection, it became very clear to me that the reason I struggled with firing people was that I did not feel comfortable with confrontation.

I am the youngest of four children and somehow was designated as the peacekeeper in my family. When I observed confrontations in my family, I typically tried to smooth things over. In retrospect, I never truly enjoyed that role. In most cases, given the option, I would try to avoid any difficult conversations or uncomfortable situations. As you might imagine, this was not a good character trait for a physician, but it was even worse for an aspiring leader.

To understand how I was able to deal with the challenge of firing people and that difficult but inevitable confrontation, I need to share two stories that, upon reflection, provided me with the building blocks to address this leadership challenge and ultimately help me grow the organizational culture I was looking for.

In the fall of 1994, I had just started my first real job, working as a primary care physician in Western Massachusetts. My wife and I had just moved from Hanover, New Hampshire, and she was pregnant with our first child. I had completed my training at Dartmouth Hitchcock Medical Center and was very excited to be putting my training into action. I was also happy to receive a real paycheck.

On my third day, I walked into an exam room to see a new patient who was about twenty-five years old with a chief complaint of "white stuff" on his tongue. I introduced myself, and we took a few moments to get to know each other. He was recently married and had a child who was less than two years old. We talked for a while about the joys and challenges of being a parent, and I shared that I was soon to be a father. In those first few minutes, we developed a connection, and I was looking forward to being his primary care physician.

After a few minutes, we started to discuss why he had come to see me. He noted that there was a white coating on his tongue and that there was a little bit of discomfort when he swallowed. Other than that, he felt well and noted no other issues. I asked him to sit on the exam table as I put on my white coat. It seems odd now that I took the time to put on my "doctor's coat", but that was the tradition back then, and I did not buck the trend. I asked him to open his mouth and quickly saw the issue - he had thrush, the medical term for a yeast infection on his tongue. This is not an uncommon finding and can often be seen after someone takes a course of antibiotics. Unfortunately, he had not taken any antibiotics, and there was no other obvious explanation.

As a new doctor, I was especially thorough and decided to order a bunch of blood work. I then prescribed treatment for the yeast infection and told him there was nothing to worry about and that I would get back to him in a few days with the results of the testing. These reassuring words were what I would now call "a rookie mistake". He was very grateful, and we both went about our days.

I received the results of the labs about two days later. He was positive for HIV/AIDS and had a CD4 count of 8. While fully understanding a CD4 count is not essential for this story, it's vital to grasp that a normal CD4 count is well over 200. In other words, this young, seemingly healthy man, recently married with a very young daughter, had advanced AIDS.

In 1994, HIV/AIDS was one of the most significant public health issues confronting our society, and a tremendous amount of anger, confusion, and misinformation surrounded this life-threatening illness. In addition, for years, there was no effective treatment. Simply put, AIDS was a death sentence.

When I saw the results, I knew that my patient was in a grave situation. In my training, I had a genuine interest in infectious diseases and was well-versed in the prognosis of someone with advanced AIDS. He had six months to live if he was lucky. I knew I had to tell him, but I felt utterly unprepared for how to share this news.

It is strange to look back now and relive my feelings and emotions from over three decades ago, but they still resonate with me to this day. I remember thinking that someone else should give him this diagnosis and prognosis. I was a mere primary care physician; all the bad news was supposed to come from a specialist, such as a cancer doctor or an infectious disease specialist. I had envisioned my role as someone who informed people that they were overweight or had high blood pressure, not that they had six months to live. It is a little-known secret in healthcare that primary care physicians are often the ones who provide the initial bad news. It is also a fact that, at least when I was in training, no one taught me how to deliver bad news.

The next day, my receptionist reached out to the patient and asked him to come in to see me at the end of the day for a follow-up. I remember being distracted all day long, thinking about the impending conversation. I also remember standing outside the exam room door, my legs shaking, almost too frightened to enter the room. I wish I could tell you that I remember the details of the conversation, but I don't. I also wish that I could tell you that I handled the conversation adeptly and had all the answers, but that would not be true. What I can tell you is that, after I gave him the results, he reached out to me and hugged me, and we cried together. I don't think I will ever forget that moment of pain and connection.

Although it is unrelated to my larger point, I want to share that a new drug called AZT had just entered the market at the time of his AIDS diagnosis. He was able to start this treatment, and against all odds, he responded beautifully. My initial prognosis was wrong; he has lived a full life.

My second story occurred about fifteen years later in my medical career. It is a painful story to share, as it involves one of my closest friends, Joyce, but I am sure she would be okay with me sharing it. She always cared about educating others, and I believe she would be thrilled if her story could positively impact someone else.

It was just a typical day at the office when I received a phone call from her. She was experiencing some acute right-sided back pain and was hoping that I could fit her into my schedule. I did not hesitate; I was absolutely going to find time to help one of my closest friends. Her complaint seemed relatively innocuous, and I didn't think it would take much time out of my day.

A few hours later, Joyce arrived at the office and was placed in an exam room along with her husband. This was a pleasant surprise because he was also a very close friend, and it gave me a few moments to relax and catch up with both of them. After a few minutes of neighborhood gossip, we got down to business.

Joyce shared her medical concerns with me. Afterwards, I conducted a thorough examination and tested her urine, looking for a potential infection. It did not show an infection, but it did reveal blood. Connecting her right-sided back pain with her bloody urine, I confidently shared that I thought she had a kidney stone and that there was nothing to worry about. I suggested an abdominal CT scan to confirm her diagnosis as a formality. You'd think that, after years in medical practice,

I would have learned a bit more humility and avoided the trap of diagnostic premature closure.

Joyce went for her CT scan, which I knew would take a few hours, and I went forward with the rest of my day. I was sitting in my office in between patients when my phone rang. The radiologist on call wanted to speak to me about the CT scan I had ordered. This was not unusual, as radiologists often needed me to modify my order or add additional testing. Since the radiology department was right below my office, I decided to walk down to their office and speak with them directly.

As I entered the radiologist's office, I could tell immediately that something was not right. The radiologist looked at me and verified that I was the ordering physician for the abdominal CT scan. I affirmed that I was, as I had just wanted to confirm the presence of a kidney stone before referring Joyce to a urologist. The radiologist paused before sharing the findings with me; it showed multiple masses in the liver and enlarged lymph nodes throughout the abdomen. Joyce had widely disseminated cancer.

There are certain moments in your life that you know will define your existence on this earth. Many of those moments are joyous, like the birth of a child, an acceptance to college, or a hole-in-one in golf (I have never had one, but I can imagine). Then there are the devastating moments like the death of a family member or knowing you are going to have to tell one of your best friends that they have metastatic cancer. When I learned of Joyce's CT findings, the whole world slowed down for a moment, and I struggled to catch my breath. I heard the radiologist talking, but I wasn't absorbing additional information. I continued to look at the images on the screen, trying to process what I medically understood but personally could not accept.

After finishing my discussion with the radiologist, I stepped outside to catch my breath and think about what I was going to say. I remember having similar feelings to the ones I had experienced the first week on the job. Why do I have to be the one to share the bad news? I am just a PCP; shouldn't someone else be sharing this diagnosis and prognosis? How am I possibly going to share this information and maintain a modicum of professionalism? Why did I not listen to my colleagues when they said not to treat your family or friends?

After completing my pity party, I returned to my office. Joyce and her husband had already been placed in an exam room to hear the results from me. Once again, I found myself standing outside an exam room with my legs shaking, and I searched for the right words. After fifteen years, I had gained a lot more experience in providing bad news, but I am not sure I was any better at it. I took a deep breath and entered the room.

The experience of providing bad news is not like it is portrayed in the movies. It is heart-wrenching and deeply painful for everyone involved. I slowly entered the room and sat down on the stool, moved close to Joyce, reached out to hold her hand, looked her in the eyes, and gave her the diagnosis. The details of the conversation have faded from my memory over the years, but I still recall that we all cried and shared several loving embraces.

I share these two stories because they have a common thread that has helped me in managing difficult situations and confrontations. I would be thrilled if the common thread was that I was tremendously skilled at providing bad news. Unfortunately, despite over three decades of experience, I am not sure I have become a subject matter expert. However, what I have found is that the key factor in addressing challenging conversations is empathy. Both stories reveal my genuine connection to the people who were confronted with an unexpected, devastating diagnosis. You don't need to cry, as I did, to express this empathy. However, finding a meaningful way to provide a small, unexpected act of kindness and to try and live in someone else's shoes just for a moment is essential to dealing with these types of critical conversation.

This brings me back to the conversation about employee dismissal. This is a critical conversation that has been the least favorite part of my job. However, by combining the AID model ("Action", "Impact", and "Desired Outcome"), Shelley's guidance about doing what's best for all, and integrating empathy, I have a structure that allows for a meaningful and successful conversation. That is a lot of leadership talk, so let me give a real-life example.

A twenty-year employee decided all the changes going on in the office were just too much. She liked the way things used to be and refused to implement new workflows. After multiple conversations and discipline, her actions remained unchanged. In fact, she decided that she disagreed with the blood pressure measurement process and just "made up" the numbers on several patients. She was a long-term employee and was beloved by many members of the staff.

My critical conversation with her started with the AID model. Along with the Director of Human Resources, we shared with her the specific actions that were leading to her dismissal. We then clearly identified the impact of her actions on the patients, the staff, and the organization. This was a compelling, integral part of any dismissal conversation. It was at this point that the conversation intentionally shifted. I made eye contact with the employee and said, "Thank you so much for your service to our organization. You have truly made a difference in the lives of patients and your colleagues. I am so sorry that this is no longer a good fit for you, but I honestly believe that leaving our organization will give you the chance to find an opportunity that once again will bring joy to your work life."

You may be saying to yourself that this approach would not work for you. And you may be right. To make any of this work, the words must be your own; you must express genuine empathy. This is only effective if you really mean it. If your comments come across as cold and stiff, you will fail, and the dismissal will be very challenging.

Now that we have discussed how to effectively move people out of your organization, you must endeavor to make that happen. So, here is another moment that you may want to dog-ear the page. You will never develop the organizational culture you want unless you identify the Bottom 15% and either move them into the Middle 70% or remove them from your organization. If you avoid this key activity to avoid confrontation and critical conversations, you will destroy your culture. Inaction is a critical failure of leadership; everyone is watching you.

6

A Cup of Tea

"Sometimes it takes only one act of kindness to change a person's life."

Jackie Chen

My friend Joyce is no longer with us. She passed away many years ago after a prolonged cancer battle. As I have thought about this book, a story that she shared during her chemotherapy treatments resurfaced for me. It is a simple story that illustrates a crucial aspect of leadership and culture.

It was a cool evening, and I had walked down the street to visit Joyce and her husband. She was in the middle of her cancer treatments and was really starting to experience the side effects of her chemotherapy. Since Joyce was not only my patient and friend but my neighbor, visiting her in the evenings was a logistically easy and emotionally comforting way to spend the evenings.

As we sat on her back deck with a few candles illuminating the darkness, I asked her a few questions about her day. She provided some perfunctory responses, and I followed up with a more in-depth question: "Has there been anything positive or memorable about your cancer journey?" Since I was in a leadership role, I was hoping she could provide me with some insight into what we were doing well as an organization. It is also possible that I was hoping she might say something positive about her primary care physician, who, at the time, was me.

Joyce did not hesitate with her response. She said, "My most memorable positive experience was a cup of hot Lipton Tea". At first, I thought she was joking, but by the look on her face, I could tell she was serious. I paused and asked her to provide a few more details behind the cup of tea.

Joyce took a moment and then began. As I noted above, Joyce was receiving chemotherapy to treat her underlying cancer. She would arrive at the oncologist's office early in the morning, and she would receive an infusion of her chemotherapy drugs. The infusions would often last several hours. The room was cool, and this, combined with the effect of her intravenous fluids and medications, made her feel very cold.

One day, as she was nearing the end of her treatment for that morning, the cold was particularly bothersome. She noted to me that she did not share her concerns with the nurse, figuring she would just finish the treatment and warm up afterwards. When she looked up a few moments later, however, the nurse handed her a Styrofoam cup. In the cup was some hot water and a Lipton tea bag. Joyce took the cup, steeped it for two more minutes, and drank it slowly. All the time, she was thinking how incredibly thoughtful this gesture was.

Joyce finished her story. "Seriously?" I replied. "After all the interactions you've had with physicians, technologists, receptionists, and me -- this is the one that stands out?" She paused and responded in a way that will always touch my heart, "I am appreciative of everyone who has helped me through these difficult times, but this small, random act of kindness was genuine, unexpected, and made me feel like she was thinking of me as a person and not as a patient".

Could it be that simple? Could it be that small, random acts of kindness represent the cornerstone of an organization's culture? Could it be that the simple act of providing someone with a lukewarm cup of tea in a 10-cent Styrofoam cup is the hidden key to organizational success?

The standard answer to this type of question is "Of course not!". Life is complicated, and there is no one simple solution. Organizational culture is complicated, and to think there is a straightforward solution is ridiculous. I agree that it sounds ridiculous. I recognize that, if this is indeed the answer, it could render the rest of the book unnecessary – yet I can't help but ask: could simple, random acts of kindness be the most essential element of organizational culture?

On a warm day a couple of years ago, I was running a little late for work as I walked towards the office entryway. As I entered the building, I saw out of the corner of my eye a woman walking towards the entrance. I did not recognize her, and she was far enough away that I could have entered the building and pretended I hadn't seen her.

Everyone knows the awkward calculation that you make at a public entrance. Do you hold the door for a stranger or put your head down and ignore the world around you? For whatever reason, I decided to hold the door open for this stranger. She was a little further away from the door than I initially calculated, which made the wait a little awkward. The young woman saw me holding the door and started to walk a little bit faster.

As she entered the building, she said a simple thank you. I could tell that she was genuinely moved by the simple gesture of a stranger holding the door for her. I didn't give the incident much thought at the time and went about my day.

In my leadership role, I tried to interact with everyone in my organization at least once a year. Many of the employees were nurses, and I typically drove to their clinical offices to meet with them. These meetings tended to be very casual and were intended to ensure that I stay connected to the organization's real work. ("staying connected" to your organization is something we will cover to a greater degree later in this book.)

In late 2022, I made a routine visit with one of the relatively new nurse care coordinators. I hadn't had the chance to meet her during her orientation, so I was excited about this opportunity. When I entered her office, she smiled and said, "Hello, Dr. Shuman, do you recognize me?" I must admit this is one of my least favorite questions. A physician meets thousands of patients, and a physician leader may interact with equally large numbers of staff. I have a terrible memory when it comes to faces, names, and just about any other defining characteristic, so I can't remember everyone. Oddly, I do have the ability to remember individuals' medical issues, even if I can't necessarily remember their names. It is not a particularly helpful skill because you cannot simply walk up to someone and say, "Hey, I know you, you are the gentleman with the big prostate."

To get back to the story, I smiled at the nurse whom I was visiting and said, "I am sorry, but I don't remember where we met before." I could tell she was a little disappointed, but she quickly recovered and said, "At the front door of the administrative office." I must admit that this was not a very helpful clue, which made me even a little more uncomfortable. Instead of responding, I remained quiet, hoping that she would provide more details. After a few seconds, which seemed like a few minutes, she continued, "I was coming for my initial interview, and you held the door for me. I didn't know who you were, and you didn't know me, but you held the door for me anyway."

That door-holding event had happened months before this interaction, but for some reason, I remembered it. She went on to tell me that, before her interview started, she shared with her interviewer that she had no problem finding the building and that a nice man in a suit jacket had held the door for her at the entrance. The interviewer said, "Oh, that was our CEO, Dr. Shuman. I saw you walk in the building with him."

The nurse now looked at me and said, "When I found out that it was the CEO of the company who had held the door for me, I knew I wanted to work here. A leader who takes a moment to hold the door for a stranger reflects the kind of thoughtful culture I want to belong to."

As I look back on this simple event, it reinforces the question, "Can simple acts of kindness be the defining characteristic of organizational culture?" I think the answer to this question is "yes". In fact, I believe that small, unexpected acts have a significantly greater impact than large ones.

Let me provide a few examples to make my point. Imagine it is your birthday. Your spouse and family gather around and buy you a cake and get you presents. In fact, they may have asked you beforehand what you might want, and you provided them with a list. The party was lovely, and you appreciate the kindness shown by your family and friends.

Now imagine this scenario. You are not feeling well and need to stay home from work. You reach out to your manager, and they express their concern. A little later, there is a knock on your door. Your manager has asked a local restaurant to deliver chicken soup to your house. You're surprised and sincerely thankful.

In both examples, individuals were thinking of you and showing you a degree of kindness. Yet I would suggest that the latter example, with the chicken soup, has a much more significant impact. Both represent small acts of kindness, but the unexpected nature of the latter example is likely to have a longer-lasting effect.

Many organizations try to "plan" culture. They create field trips, charitable events, holiday parties, and team-building activities. These planned events are important, but they are not sufficient to build culture. As I noted previously, many of the most impactful moments are small and seem insignificant at the time. Opening a door, sharing a cup of tea, remembering a colleague's birthday, visiting a colleague's cubicle to check in on them, making a pie for friends, and listening intently are all small acts of kindness. If, as a leader, you can promote this culture of kindness, you are likely to have a tremendously successful organization.

The question remains: how do you create a culture where employees genuinely want to be kind to one another? Although there are certainly some things leadership can do to promote these types of behaviors, it ultimately comes from the hiring process. If you focus on hiring people who are humble, hardworking, emotionally intelligent, and joyful, it is very likely that these will be the same people who embrace small acts of kindness. You must serve as an example and live this value.

The first thing I would suggest is to review your organization's mission, vision, and, most importantly, guiding principles. As I shared earlier, in my last organization, employees created these principles, which helped ensure their buy-in. I share them again here because I think they are worth repeating:

1. ***Compassion***: We intentionally perform acts of kindness
2. ***Teamwork***: We speak with and for each other, not against each other
3. ***Leadership***: We act with integrity and humility

4. ***Personal Integrity***: We advocate for others as if they were our family
5. ***Accountability***: We own our decisions and our work

The second thing I would suggest is that you live by these values, not just espouse them. I can't tell you how many organizations come up with a great mission, a solid vision, and strong guiding principles that just sit on a shelf and gather dust. Perhaps even worse, they create these essential documents but choose to ignore them when making organizational decisions. It is inexcusable as a leader not to live your values. By failing to do so, you will never build a thriving organizational culture, and you will not be respected as a leader.

There are many ways to live your values, especially if one of them is to perform small, random acts of kindness. I have provided several examples, but I would like to revisit a framework that might make success even easier. As I have noted previously, I like to use the AID (Action/Impact/Desired Outcome) framework when providing feedback. Most leaders use this model to share disciplinary news. I have found that it can be invaluable when building organizational culture and living your values.

A simple example is that of a staff member who bakes some food for their colleagues and brings it into the office. Everybody loves food, so this clearly qualifies as a small, unexpected act of kindness. In most cases, the individual receives appreciation from their colleagues, and the day continues. I would suggest you take such an opportunity to use the AID model to reinforce your guiding principles. You might consider saying the following, "Hi, Donna, I just wanted to thank you for bringing in that blueberry pie. It tastes amazing! I also wanted to acknowledge the meaningful impact of your taking the time to prepare food for colleagues. It creates an environment where we perform kind acts for one another. It makes this organization a better place to work. I can't thank you enough for living our values. I love blueberry pie, so please don't hesitate to make some more!"

I know it sounds a little corny, but I want to emphasize the importance of providing positive feedback along with an impact statement. It also helps to emphasize the desired outcome. In the example above, I have hit on the three aspects of the AID model:

> **Action:**
> Baking a blueberry pie for her colleagues
> **Impact:**
> Lives our values and improves the work environment
> **Outcome:**
> Creates a culture of kindness (and maybe I get more pie in the future)

You will be amazed at the impact it will make on your culture if you take the time every day to identify a positive act at your work and apply the AID model. Not only will it impact the specific employee, but others will also notice it. It will influence their attitude and behavior. In addition, it has one other unexpected impact: it will make you a happier person at work. As a leader, you often spend your time putting out fires or dealing with disgruntled employees. If you spend a lot of your time dealing with the bottom 15%, it can be emotionally draining. On the other hand, when you acknowledge positive behavior, it can truly lift your spirits.

As my son is an actor, I often find myself looking for an excuse to visit him and watch a Broadway show. One time several years ago, we had the opportunity to watch a Broadway musical called "Come from Away". It is a fantastic musical about the events of September 11, 2001, as viewed from the perspective of a small town in Newfoundland called Gander. It is a must-see/read.

The play, based on a true story, relives the events of 9/11 and reminds us that all air traffic in the United States on that day came to a halt, requiring many planes to make emergency landings. One of the places where many planes landed was an airport in Newfoundland. The story depicts how the passengers, forced to spend several days in this small town, interacted with the townspeople and how incredibly generous the people of Gander were with these strangers. At the end, one of the stranded passengers resolves to remember 9/11 not for the terrible events of the day but for the incredible generosity he encountered from strangers. He puts this remembrance into action by providing each of his employees with $100 every September 11th that they may use to perform a small, random act of kindness for a stranger.

I found this gesture to be incredibly touching. I stole this idea, and every September 11th, I provided members of my Senior Leadership Team with $100. I only asked that they use this money to perform a small, random act of kindness for a stranger. The first year I did this, the leaders were speechless. They asked how they could use the money and whether they needed to provide a report on how they used it. I replied that I trusted them to "do the right thing"; there was to be no reporting.

Nevertheless, these leaders were so excited about the impact of their actions that they couldn't help but subsequently share their stories. They talked about providing clothes for homeless children, supporting domestic abuse shelters, and providing Christmas gifts for children of underserved families. They shared with me that this opportunity made them feel good about their workplace and proved that we were committed to living our values. Equally important, they wanted to cascade this tradition to others in the organization. It was a moment when I realized that small acts of kindness could truly shape an organizational culture.

There is a moment in many books where they seem to take a tangent, such as a long description of a landscape or perhaps a thoughtful recollection of a city. That moment is about to happen here. I am going to stray from this book's topic, organizational culture, to a much larger topic: "What is the meaning of life?" Bear with me for just a few paragraphs, as there is a connection between this question and the rest of this chapter and this book.

Recently, I was wasting some time on social media and came across a brief video in which a woman was saying the following: "Have you ever thought about this? In 100 years, we will all be buried with our family and friends. Strangers will live in the homes that we worked so hard to build, and someone else will own everything we own today. Our descendants will hardly know who we were. After we die, we will be remembered for a few more years, and then we will become just a portrait on someone's wall."

The video goes on to remind us that we should not worry so much about life's day-to-day stressors. I am not a huge fan of grand-scale existentialism, but it did make me think about the larger question: "If life is short and we will ultimately not be remembered unless we are famous or powerful, what should we focus on during our time here? What would create a meaningful life?"

As I enter my early sixties I have struggled with this question. Minds much greater than my own have struggled with the concept of legacy and life's meaning for centuries. Despite that caveat, I would like to offer my perspective: I believe that what gives our lives meaning is the kindness we show to others. I am not talking about grand gestures but small, everyday acts of kindness. This includes listening intently to someone's story, holding the door open for them, buying a friend a cup of coffee, or simply sending a text to let someone know you are thinking about them.

These acts of kindness create a ripple effect that can have a lasting impact well beyond your awareness and extend far beyond your lifetime. The concept of "paying forward" a kindness is not a new one. However, I think the idea of tying that small act of kindness to our greater purpose is novel. As I conclude this tangent, I would like to emphasize that the small, random acts of kindness that are essential in building an organizational culture will likely have a much broader impact than one might initially imagine.

7

Resilience

"Do not judge me by my successes, judge me by how many times I fell down and got back up again."

Nelson Mandela

It was my first week in the urgent care clinic during my residency. I was both super excited and tremendously nervous as I saw patients on my own for the first time. Even though an experienced physician was serving as a backup, I felt a surge of energy and independence.

Most of my days were spent seeing patients with standard urgent care problems such as colds, sore throats, back pain, and headaches. I remember a young gentleman who came to see me with a chief complaint of dizziness. I did a basic evaluation and confidently diagnosed him with a viral inner ear infection and provided him with some medications and symptom management instructions. It was just another simple visit with a simple treatment for a burgeoning Marcus

Welby, MD. (This is a reference to a classic TV show about a well-respected physician.)

Two weeks later, the patient returned; his symptoms persisted. He was dizzy, nauseated, and had an intense headache. His difficulty with walking had now become much more pronounced. I asked the supervising physician to examine this patient. He performed a thorough examination, viewing the patient's retinas (the back of the eyes) with an ophthalmoscope (an eye device). After completing the exam, he asked me to step out of the examination room. He noted to me that the patient had swelling of his optic discs, and he needed a CT scan.

A couple of hours later, the CT scan was completed, and the patient's diagnosis became very clear; he had a large brain tumor. I remember that moment to this day. My stomach hurt, I couldn't breathe, and I just wanted to hide in a dark room. I had failed to make the diagnosis when the patient had initially seen me. This person had entrusted me with their health, and I had let them down. I felt that I was an inept doctor and that I needed to reconsider my career choice. The patient died less than 6 months later, leaving behind a wife and two children.

Becoming a physician is a long and arduous road. The stress starts out as a mental and intellectual challenge, progresses to a physical marathon, and ultimately becomes a lifelong responsibility to, as Hippocrates said, "first, do no harm". It is an unspoken truth that physicians constantly live with the risk of making a mistake that will result in permanent injury or death to another human being. Sadly, the saying "At least no one died" often doesn't hold true for physicians.

This was not the only mistake I made as a physician. Like every clinician who spends thirty years caring for patients, I encountered moments when my judgment fell short. However, what I learned over that period is that being a good physician has a lot more to do with relationships than it does intellectual prowess. Please understand me - you need to be a subject matter expert to be a good clinician, but a knowledge base is far from sufficient.

I had the honor of teaching students throughout my career and on the first day of their rotation with me, I would always ask them the same question: "When you come out of the examination room, I want you to tell me if the patient is sick or not." The students would always look at me with a confused look but would oblige me. Often, they would come out of the patient room, usually an hour later, and tell me that the patient was sick. That was hardly ever the case.

Over the course of their rotations with me, they started to develop a sense of illness severity as they began to combine knowledge with real-life experience. They started to understand that two people could have the same diagnosis but based on their support network and home situation, could be experiencing illness in a completely different way. Ultimately, they learned that the only way to be a great physician was to have an authentic relationship with their patients, allowing them to use their diagnostic skills effectively.

Just like the students, I learned to accept that I would make mistakes, but I also needed to be resilient and develop meaningful relationships with my patients. In this way, when someone whom I thought was only mildly ill turned out to be very sick, they would feel enough of a connection with me that they would reach out to me quickly, and we could correct the course. Knowledge, relationships, failure, and resilience turned out to be the keys to being a successful doctor. Interestingly, it is these same characteristics that result in great leaders and the development of meaningful organizational culture.

Let's focus on the concept of failure. Organizations fail all the time. Ideas that seemed great at the time often turn out to be "clunkers." The list of bad ideas I have had is endless.

In fact, the joke in one of my organizations was that "I don't have any good ideas, but I am great at operationalizing other people's ideas". I was okay with this organizational belief since it reinforced the ethos that everyone contributed to making things better and that we were not a top-down organization.

I have always liked the expression that if you are not trying and failing, then you are not trying hard enough. Yet, in my experience, it is rare for organizations not to have new ideas. In fact, there are typically so many new ideas that it has spawned a new consulting line of business called "change management." (I am amazed that we pay people who don't know our employees and know nothing about our business to come in and tell us how to reassure our employees that "change is good") It is not a dearth of ideas that is the issue; it is the unwillingness of organizations to admit that their great idea was not so great after all. Months and often years go by until it becomes evident to everyone that it is time to throw in the towel. Sometimes the greatest failure is not admitting defeat in a timely manner.

Great organizations have a culture that puts processes in place to evaluate strategic success and failures on a regular basis. That last sentence sounds like corporate lingo so let me try again. Sit with your friends regularly and take joy in your achievements and admit when you screwed up. Be honest with each other and include the CEO. Ask the employees in the trenches if things are working and be sincere about wanting their input. I promise you they will tell you if your ideas are not achieving your well-intended purpose.

Ok, so now you know - your idea was a complete failure. Sometimes, failures occur on a small scale and other times they are out there for everyone to see. I have often wanted to hold a conference of leaders and have them share their greatest failures. I think I could learn a lot from that type of conference, but I am concerned that leaders would be loath to share failures. They might only present stories that show them in a good light, such as those stories that say they failed because they were simply too generous to their employees.

Regardless, take some time to understand why you have failed. Was the idea a poor idea? Was it a good idea but poorly timed? Was it a great idea poorly operationalized? Please take some time with your leaders to focus on your failures and not just your successes. Once you have completed that important task, it is time to move your organization forward and reinforce one of the most important parts of organizational culture: resilience.

One of the great writers of our time, Doris Kearns Goodwin, wrote Leadership in Turbulent Times, a book about four of our greatest presidents. She explores the presidencies of Abraham Lincoln, Teddy Roosevelt, Franklin Roosevelt, and Lyndon Johnson and how they responded to challenges during their terms. In 2018, she was interviewed by Judy Woodruff from the PBS NewsHour about her book. Woodruff asked Kearns, "why she focused on the early lives of these presidents and their failures?" Kearns responded:

> "In people who've been through difficult times in their lives, through adversities, and come through with resilience, there is a strength and a wisdom. They have learned from their mistakes. They have learned from what fate might deal them.
>
> I mean, Lincoln had a near suicidal depression when he felt like he had broken his word to his constituencies, broken his promise to Mary that he would get married to her. And they had to take all knives and razors and scissors from his room. But he comes out of that by saying, "I would just as soon die now, but I have not yet accomplished anything to make any human being remember that I have lived," incredible, right?

> Teddy Roosevelt loses his wife and his mother on the same day in the same house. He goes to the Badlands. He rides his horse 15 hours a day. But by being in the West, he absorbs this love of nature, and he becomes a Westerner, as well as an Easterner.
>
> FDR, of course, has his polio. And when he took up that rehab center in Warm Springs, and he was Doc Roosevelt to his fellow polio patients, he taught them how to live again, a life of joy, even if they were paralyzed. It's exactly what he was able to do with the country when the country was paralyzed.
>
> LBJ has a massive heart attack when he's on the top of the heap as majority leader, but he says, what if I died now? What would I be remembered for? And then he goes right for civil rights in the Senate, goes right for civil rights in the presidency.
>
> So, something happens, I think, when you go through a hard time. You come through it with resilience, a really important quality. It doesn't have to be as harrowing as these guys had. But it has to be something."

Woodruff then followed up by asking, "You describe the adversity, but is there some secret sauce, some magic formula that we should learn from what they went through? Because some people look at this, and they say, "I want to know, what is—what's the magic formula?". Kearns responded:

> "There is no magic trick. In fact, there's no clear trajectory for any of them to reach the top of the presidency. There's a family resemblance of traits, I would argue. I think humility is one of them. Empathy. If you can develop empathy, even if you're

> not born with it, is another one. Resilience, as we have just been talking about. Self-reflection, being able to acknowledge errors. Build a team that you can share credit with, and you can shoulder blame if something goes wrong. Learning how to communicate with people. But, most important, at some point, ambition for the self-became ambition for something larger. And that's what united all of these disparate characters."

I realize that being a leader of a healthcare institution is a far cry from being the President of the United States. However, the concepts of humility, resilience, empathy, self-reflection, and a greater purpose should resonate with all organizational leaders. I will touch on most of these topics throughout the book. Let's focus on resilience for a moment.

There are so many times in one's life when the unexpected happens and you are left with a sense of frustration, anger, and often sadness. This happened to me when I was finishing my medical training in my late twenties.

I was in my third year of internal medicine training at Dartmouth Hitchcock Medical Center in Hanover, New Hampshire. As I have described previously, medical training is a grueling adventure with incredible highs and tremendous lows. In many ways, the first two years of internal medicine residency are the most difficult with the third year reserved for a greater leadership and teaching role. As I entered that third year, I was very excited since I had truly bonded with my colleagues and I had met the love of my life, Elie, a bone marrow transplant nurse whom I had recently married.

Then it happened with no real warning. I woke up one morning and simply felt tired and sad. I didn't think too much about it, and I started my daily routine and went to work. Unfortunately, the feeling didn't go away. I started to feel anxious, and the sadness started to feel a little heavier. I went to bed early that day, thinking that a good night's sleep would solve my emotional issues. I was wrong.

This event happened over thirty years ago, so the details are a little fuzzy. The memory of the physical feelings, however, has never dissipated. Over the next several months, I fell into a deep depression. I awoke with a low-grade nausea that persisted over the entire day. I had no energy and no interest in doing anything. I clearly remember thinking, "I don't think I will ever feel better". The minutes were long, the hours were painful, and the days were unbearable. Although I never considered hurting myself, I was experiencing a relentless sense of hopelessness. I eventually pursued counseling, meditation, and medical therapy. I spent days writing in my journal and spending time in self-reflection. I focused on my youth and the conflicts I had with my parents. I was in a very dark place, and the only light came from my friends, my siblings, and my wife.

I wish I could say that there was a revelation that led to my quick recovery but that would not be true. Recovering from a major depression is not like flipping a light switch. It was a gradual process that slowly allowed me to feel less hopeless. I began to feel less nauseous, and joy gradually crept into my subconscious. However, as a physician, I knew that depression was a chronic illness often characterized by recurrence. I was encouraged by progress but lived in fear of the potential darkness of an unknown future.

When I finally recovered enough to return to work, I was hesitant and scared. I was fortunate to have a tremendous support network and over time, I was able to complete my medical training. For those who are reading this book and have experienced depression, you will understand the long journey to recovery. You may also understand that depression often returns. I have certainly had times in my life where I have experienced similar but milder symptoms. I take those moments to remember my initial episode and that, despite how I feel in the moment, there will be light again. I also look back at those times and feel a sense of pride. The ability to be resilient in the face of fear and uncertainty was something I did not associate with my personality. I wish I could share a point of wisdom that would help others navigate depression, but I do know that the experience I lived through gave me the perspective I needed to be a better doctor, a better husband, a better friend, a better father, and a better leader.

In running an organization, the concept of resilience is slightly different but equally important. I have experienced leaders who confuse resilience with recalcitrance. They feel that if something is not working, persistence alone will lead to success. They believe that their vision is correct, do not have enough humility to accept their failures, and drive an organization in the wrong direction.

Organizational resilience should look very similar to personal resilience. It is grounded in understanding your failures, accepting them, and moving ahead. You need to understand the experience of failure but be willing to take new chances going forward. Use the opportunity to hear new voices and be open to change. Keep moving forward and confronting the darkness, remembering that you've been here before—and that the way out can be so extraordinary, it's worth the risk.

8

Tigger

"I think it is a shame that so many people live and die with the music still in them .... We spend so much of our time working, why not have fun at it?"

Robert Beck

You must be asking why a book about organizational culture has a chapter named after a fictional animal named Tigger. The answer lies with a woman I met many years ago when I just started seeing patients in Western Massachusetts. I will never forget the interaction because it has impacted my life for decades. She entered the room accompanied by her husband for a routine blood pressure check in early October. She was a lovely person, and we immediately connected on a personal level. She told me about her life and her children, and the visit went way past the scheduled fifteen minutes.

Towards the end of the appointment, she asked me, "Are you going to dress up for Halloween?" I didn't have a great answer and simply replied, "I hadn't really thought about it, but I do have an adult-sized Tigger costume that I bought from the Disney Store. I was thinking of wearing it while trick-or-treating with my kids." She paused, then asked, "Why don't you wear it to work on Halloween?" I hesitated. "I'm not sure that's a great idea," I said. She smiled and finished the conversation with, "I tell you what—if you come into work dressed as Tigger on Halloween, I'll make you a new costume every year from the Hundred Acre Wood until you have all the characters." I smiled at her and nodded.

As Halloween approached, I experienced reservations about my agreement, but I had made a promise, and I wasn't going to step away from my commitment. In addition, she had been leaving me messages saying that she was going to come in for a blood pressure check on Halloween and would be looking for me in costume. So, on October 31st, I slipped into a full-sized Tigger outfit and drove into work as a 6-foot Disney character with a voice recording that bellowed "Oh-Oh-Oh-Oh-I'm Tigger" every time I pressed the button sewn into the hand of the costume.

As I exited my car and walked toward the office, there she was waiting for me. She exclaimed, "I wasn't sure that you were going to do it, but I am so glad you did". I proceeded into the building and was met by a combination of laughter and amazement. I was a little embarrassed but continued down the hall to the clinical pod where I saw patients and then spent the entire day in the costume. Patients who knew me just laughed, but new patients were a little more uncertain about putting their confidence in a large furry creature. In between patients, I visited different departments and especially enjoyed my time in Pediatrics. I was certainly not the only person in the office dressed for Halloween, but I was the only senior leader who took the leap.

After the day passed, I did not think much of it. A few months later, that patient returned for a routine visit. She noted that she had been a seamstress her entire life and was ready to make good on our bet. She was going to start by making me an Eeyore costume. I smiled and told her it was not necessary, but she insisted. Several months later, just before Halloween, she showed up to the office with a six-foot-tall donkey costume. I tried it on and found that I looked just like Eeyore. It was amazing, and I received rave reviews when I wore it that Halloween.

For many years after that, I received a new costume: Winnie the Pooh, Kanga, Roo, Piglet, and Owl. It became a tradition to wear these to the office but also around the neighborhood. My wife and children (as they got older) would also wear the costumes and bring smiles to many faces.

It really did not occur to me at the time the impact these costumes had on my success as a leader. It turns out that vulnerability is a very powerful leadership tool. It reveals you as human to your employees and creates a dynamic in which you are more approachable. The costumes also made people laugh, reminding us all of the importance of encouraging joy at work. In a previous chapter, I referred to joy as one of the characteristics that should be integral to your hiring practices since it is essential in building a culture. Perhaps you should ask people in the interview process if they dress up for Halloween? I know it sounds crazy, but the willingness to be vulnerable and the desire to bring joy to others are key aspects of an ideal workplace. Somehow, this is beaten out of us as we grow up, especially as we become organizational leaders. I suggest that you don't let that happen to you. Fight against the current of always being in charge and in control. Let your inner child free every once in a while.

Many years ago, I had the unfortunate circumstance of working for a challenging boss. We did not share the same values, and I struggled mightily to balance my work and personal life. After a particularly challenging day, my daughter, who was in her late teens, asked me if everything was okay. I responded with a perfunctory, "Yeah, I will be fine." Evidently, my answer was not convincing. She looked at me again and said, "I miss my 4-year-old dad". I paused as her comment soaked in; it was heart-wrenching to hear this from my daughter. I had always tried to be joyful and often that would result in me acting like a 4-year-old. I took great pride in that, and whenever I exhibited this type of immaturity, like dressing up as a six-foot-tall kangaroo from the Hundred Acre Wood, she would look at me, shake her head, and hold up four fingers as an indication of my maturity level. She has always been wise well beyond her years.

After her comment, I realized that it was time to change jobs. I had known this for a while, but sometimes small actions can have a big impact. In retrospect, it also reminds me that being joyful is essential to a great organization, whether as an employee or a leader. Take the time to find an environment that allows you to manifest that aspect of your personality. If your work environment is sullen and doesn't allow you to be vulnerable or bring joy, it is time to move on.

I would like to make one more point on this topic. A while ago, I was asked how can you evaluate someone for "joyfulness"? Earlier I noted that there is a subjectivity to joy, but I also believe that not everything is measurable. When you interact with people, trust your senses and your initial impressions. When all else fails, simply ask the person, "Are you joyful?". You will be amazed at the variety of responses you get, but it can often be tremendously enlightening.

9

Storytelling

"The most powerful person in the world is the storyteller. The storyteller sets the vision, values, and agenda of an entire generation that is to come."

Steve Jobs

Part of being a great leader and shaping organizational culture is being vulnerable. When I shared this with other leaders, I often received the classic eye roll. They reminded me of traditional, strong leaders who certainly never showed vulnerability to their employees. They talked about leadership in the armed services or large, successful organizations like Apple or Amazon. I reminded them that every situation was different and required a different set of leadership skills. I also reinforced that vulnerability should not be perceived as weakness and that financial success should not be misconstrued as organizational success.

If you accept the premise that there is value in vulnerability, does that mean you have to dress up as Piglet to connect with your employees? Obviously, the answer is no, but I know where you can get a homemade costume if you want to try it. Honestly, the best way to be vulnerable is through storytelling. It is an art form that somehow has been replaced by slide presentations and emailed documents. If you can integrate storytelling into your leadership approach, you will more effectively connect with your team and set the culture you are looking to build.

The antithesis of storytelling is a bad PowerPoint presentation. As a leader, I spent countless hours watching others share their ideas through PowerPoint slides. It is impossible to put into words how many mind-numbing presentations I have had to endure, but I am going to try. You are doing your audience a disservice if you do any of the following during your presentations:

1. Put more than 10 words on a slide
2. Read your content word-for-word
3. Project any small image or table that forces you to say "I know you can't read this but..."
4. Use a font size of less than 24 points
5. Use a light slide background
6. Talk to the slides and not the audience

I could go on, but I imagine that I have now captured the behavior of most business leaders. The question is why would you compile a boring presentation that no one can read and then read it to them verbatim from the slides? If you are going to do that, why do they need to be there? You could just send them the slide deck. If you want to learn how to put together a more engaging presentation, you might check out the TEDx talk "Death by PowerPoint". It is awesome.

In our current culture, we see many examples of storytelling. Some of the most interesting ones can be found in presentations from "The Moth" or "TED", which often share amazing stories of everyday individuals doing extraordinary things. Although their stories are compelling, the way they are presented adds genuine gravitas.

Interestingly, this important art form is not routinely taught in leadership classes. It is common for intelligent people to fail to connect with their target audience. As a result, they are ineffective in conveying their mission, vision, and purpose. I suggest considering three factors:

1. A comfort with public speaking
2. An interesting story or a common experience to share
3. A willingness to be vulnerable

It amazes me how many leaders do not like public speaking. It is even more surprising to me how many leaders have had no training in public speaking and truly struggle to run meetings or give lectures. This lack of training results in the PowerPoint failures that I have enumerated. If this applies to you, please do not despair. There is hope, but, as with most things in life, you must go through a stage of self-awareness and acceptance before you move on to self-improvement.

When my executive coach asked whether I thought I was a good public speaker, I tried to be humble, but I ultimately answered affirmatively. She suggested that we record my next public speaking event, which we would then review together. I obliged and we proceeded to watch the video together. I will never forget how uncomfortable that review session was for me. It turned out I wasn't a good public speaker, and even worse, my presentation lacked focus. I still remember her questions and insights, which included the following:

1. What is the unifying theme of your presentation?
2. Since people are likely to remember only one point from your presentation, what do you want that to be?

3. How many filler words (“um”, “ah”, “ya know”, “like”, “but”) do you think you used?
4. Why do you lean to one side when you speak?
5. Why do you speak with your hands in your pockets?
6. Why are your hand gestures so small and below your waist?
7. Why do you stare at the screen when you talk and not look people in the eyes?
8. Why are you reading your slides verbatim?
9. Why are there so many words on your slides?

I am pretty sure there were more items on the list, but you get the idea; there was a lot of room for improvement. The good news is that all these items could be fixed with some practice and effort. I eventually asked my friend, Dan, to critique my presentations. He would count my filler words and provide valuable feedback. Over time, my public speaking improved. So can yours.

The ability to communicate is an essential part of leadership. There are many different types of communication: verbal, non-verbal, written, small meetings, 1:1 meetings, etc., but they are all key to creating culture. Your ability to be a good public speaker helps set the tone for the organization. This is especially true in large organizations, where getting to know everyone individually is not feasible. Your ability to connect and be relatable in public settings is essential to your organization's success.

When I talk about storytelling, the most common response I hear is, “I don’t have any interesting stories to tell.” It would be easy—and perhaps polite—for me to accept that answer, but I don’t. I believe everyone has a story worth sharing. Our stories live in childhood memories, relationships with siblings and parents, marriages, and, especially, in our experiences as parents. We all lead lives filled with moments that have shaped us. When someone tells me they don’t have an interesting story, I don't hear a lack of experiences; I hear hesitation. More often than not, it's a quiet reluctance to be vulnerable.

In my opinion, the best leaders are willing to be vulnerable and to share a part of themselves with their employees. Like most things in life, there is a balance, and you do not want to overshare, but it is essential to show your staff that you are a real person who puts their pants on one leg at a time, just like they do.

Here was an example. Carlos Martins was the Chief Operating Officer of an organization of which I was proudly a part. He is one of the kindest, most thoughtful, and smartest leaders I had ever known. His job required him to enforce the rules and create fairness across the organization. I thought this job had many similarities to that of a vice principal at a high school. As a result, for people who did not know him personally, there was a perception of toughness that was truly unjustified. He hated the disciplinary aspects of his job and often lost hours of sleep as he tried to say just the right thing while upholding the organization's standards.

In an all-staff meeting, Carlos gave a presentation called "A Day in My Life." I knew this was going to be a difficult presentation for him since he was a private person and typically worked hard to compartmentalize his personal and professional life. This presentation required him to be vulnerable and share a little bit of himself with our entire organization. He spent a long time putting together a presentation that did not violate the PowerPoint rules that I had cited above. It was amazing. He shared stories about his love for coffee, his favorite vacation spots, his two children, and his new grandson. He let others see a side of him that, until then, only his close friends had known.

This presentation allowed him to connect with people in the organization who, until then, had never really known him. It made him a real person with interests shared by others. The most effective stories were relatable; those that spoke about a relationship with a child or pet were almost universally understandable and quickly connected him with his audience.

In another example, I was giving a lecture to a group of physicians whom I really did not know. The topic was how to code and bill for an office visit. The details don't really matter; my point is that it was going to be a necessary but painful and boring talk. Since most of the people did not know each other, name tags were required. My nametag read, "Richard Shuman, MD". At the beginning of the lecture, I recounted the following story:

> The last time I wore a name tag like this was for a similar lecture many years ago. As I was getting dressed for it, I placed the name tag on my suit. My son, who was probably six or seven at the time, asked me what the MD stood for. Like any good parent, I responded with "What do you think?" He paused and eventually said, "My Dad?" I smiled and said, "Of course. That is definitely what it stands for."

This simple story about my child was relatable to almost everyone in the audience, shared a small piece of my life, and brought laughter to the room. If you can incorporate humor into your public appearances, it can be tremendously helpful in grounding you as a leader.

Again, the final part of storytelling is a willingness to be vulnerable. When a leader shows vulnerability, they become relatable. Life is full of common experiences and, when we take the time to share a part of ourselves, it makes us much more approachable and more interesting to our colleagues. I realize that this is not the standard approach to leadership. In fact, when I started out as a leader, I rarely shared personal details about my family or my life. I focused on being very professional and addressing organizational challenges. That made me like everyone else: competent but unremarkable.

How do you show vulnerability without oversharing? This is a potential pitfall, but my general experience is that leaders tend to under share and often only talk about their personal and professional successes. To connect with your target audience, you need to share your challenges and your failures. In many ways, it comes back to humility. Sharing your failures makes you relatable since everyone has experienced challenges and failure in their lives. Sharing your failures creates a sense of vulnerability and reflects a humble leadership style.

10

Creating a Culture of Engagement and Retention

"When we tell people to do their jobs, we get workers. When we trust people to get the job done, we get leaders."

Simon Sinek

Several years ago, I attended a lecture presented by one of LinkedIn's leaders. LinkedIn is an online professional networking platform. I had low expectations for this in-person meeting but was pleasantly surprised at the quality of the information and the speaker's excellent presentation and storytelling skills. He presented several truly compelling facts about employment post-pandemic and the culture shift in the newest generation of employees.

He shared that, in 2023, the average time an employee stayed with an organization was 2.8 years. I remember hearing this statistic and being surprised by this brevity. After all, I had grown up in a generation where the goal was to join an organization, grow within it, and stay there your entire career.

Was it possible that my entire paradigm about organizational culture was wrong, that the world had changed, and that I had not kept up? Am I just a weathered physician executive with outdated views? Am I just too old?

Those are all reasonable questions and have introduced doubt into my mind as I have written this book. There is no doubt that the workplace changed after the pandemic. Remote and hybrid work are ubiquitous, and the desire for work-life balance is more pervasive now than ever. However, I think it is important to examine a trend that emerged in the medical community and is likely to have a significant impact on employment, engagement, and retention: telehealth.

During the pandemic, a significant amount of healthcare was delivered remotely. Because in-person visits were not available, medical care shifted to video visits and phone calls. In many places, more than 80% of care was delivered remotely at the height of the pandemic. This represented a dramatic shift in the healthcare delivery system, and many leaders believed that, given the convenience of remote care, we would never return to a pre-pandemic state. Those predictions proved to be both right and wrong.

In the six years since the pandemic, about 15% of all healthcare visits are provided through telehealth. This is driven predominantly by mental health visits and routine primary care visits that do not require a physical examination.

Otherwise, patients have largely returned to in-person visits in medical offices. The desire for face-to-face interaction remains strong, and we often underestimate the value of personal connection in the delivery of high-quality care. The subtleties of care are often missed over video, and a lack of personal connection can limit a patient's willingness to share important personal information.

What is happening in healthcare is a microcosm of a broader engagement issue. In general, employees seek a balance between professional and personal needs. The movement toward a fully remote environment has delivered significant benefits for many employees, but it also creates challenges in building and sustaining organizational culture. Forcing people to return to the office every day may feel familiar, but it no longer adequately meets the needs of today's workforce. A hybrid workforce represents the future, allowing organizations to develop culture while balancing the needs of both the workforce and the workplace.

In addition, a hybrid workforce allows for meaningful in-person interaction. As we have seen in healthcare, people value face-to-face connection and want to balance it with the convenience of remote life. If organizations can build cultures that genuinely support hybrid work, the current 2.8-year employment horizon might be extended to four or five years. The question then becomes, "How do we build a culture to support a hybrid workforce?"

This is the question that many organizations are currently struggling with. I find it quite interesting to listen to industry experts as they reflect on the current employment situation. The level of confidence they exhibit in such a fluid situation is perplexing. It is important to show humility and accept that we don't yet know how to create an awesome organizational culture in a hybrid workforce. Here are some essential concepts to consider:

1. Working from home is not an accommodation.
2. Assume positive intent when your staff are working from home.
3. Invest in their home workspace as you would in their office space.
4. Focus on outcomes, not on process measures.

5. If the outcomes are not met, the issue is rarely that someone is working remotely, and the solution is rarely to force that person to work in the office.
6. Understand that not all work can be done remotely and should not cascade to people in the office.
7. Out of sight should never be out of mind. Connect regularly.
8. Have clear communication expectations.
9. Be flexible, but remember that, as a leader, you must continue to make sure the needs of the organization are met.
10. Use in-person time to connect informally with your staff

During the COVID-19 pandemic, the organization I was leading needed everyone to work remotely. There really was no other option except to have everyone suddenly retreat to their homes and transition an in-person culture to an at-home working environment. It was less than ideal. Over time, however, we improved our ability to work remotely and learned how to manage videoconferencing and other key organizational functions from the comfort of our homes.

As the pandemic subsided, we began to return to the office, but it was clear that many of our employees were reluctant to return to their previous work environment. It was also clear that the world had changed; the idea of remote work was not only accepted but had become the norm for certain work functions. My leadership team and I decided to accommodate individuals who wanted to work remotely. In many ways, we felt forced to adjust since many other organizations were already providing this option, and we did not want to lose our employees. The problem with thinking of these work arrangements as "accommodations" is that this suggests that they are temporary. As a result, you fail to maximize the efficiency of these remote workers. Finally, there is often a lack of trust that these individuals are actually doing their jobs. It was not uncommon for people in the office to wonder whether remote workers were spending their workday hanging out with their children, walking in the park, doing their grocery shopping, or just watching TV.

In my opinion, it is essential to assume positive intent and trust your employees. Working a hybrid or remote schedule should not be an accommodation; it should be just part of a job description. Organizations need to build cultural expectations around this new paradigm and develop new ways of creating inclusivity. We also need to stop focusing on the process and emphasize the outcomes. If an employee is not meeting their job expectations, that is a performance issue, not a site of work issue.

I do want to apply one caveat. It is not uncommon for individuals to struggle to perform all their roles remotely. At times, they must rely on those in the office to cover the small tasks they can't manage from home. This needs to be discussed and acknowledged, sometimes as an impact on compensation. Two people can hold the same position with slightly different job descriptions, depending on their place of work, and consequently receive different salaries.

As I created the "Top Ten" list shared above, I was struck by the tenth item, the idea of connecting informally with your staff. As a leader, especially in a large organization, it can be challenging to connect informally with your staff. You tend to interact in defined meetings or when giving a public address to your organization. Although these formal interactions are essential, they are only a small component of developing an ideal business culture.

I've heard time and again from staff that it's in spontaneous, unplanned interactions where real work happens and genuine camaraderie forms. Historically, I have personally found spontaneous interactions to be the most fruitful and gratifying part of my job. The immediacy and candor that emanate from these discussions build a connection between you and your staff that is hard to replicate.

The challenge, as I see it, is how to create spontaneity, immediacy, and connection with part- or full-time remote workers? I would love to provide you with one simple answer, but factors like the personality of the remote worker, the company mission and their role in the team must be taken into consideration. Below are some ways I have found to make these workers included as part of the workplace culture.

1. Use technology to your advantage. If you are thinking about an employee, just send them a text or an email. It doesn't have to be fancy or even work related. It could be wishing them a good day or cheering on their favorite sports team. Ideally something you have in common. One of my favorite employees was a Philadelphia Eagles fan and every gameday we texted each other. It has created a special bond that continues to this day.
2. Recognize their expertise. If an employee has a particular work-related expertise that you want to know more about, set up a video call to learn from them. Creating a dynamic, even remotely, where the employee is the subject matter expert can create a very special connection.
3. Send a card. Take the time to send a card on your employees' birthday or work anniversary. I know it is time consuming, but a personal written card creates a magical connection. Very few leaders reach out to their employees in such a personal way but the ones that do create a culture which is special and transcends the gap of the remote workplace

In a later chapter we are going to talk about listening skills as a leader but for now I think it is important to emphasize that great leaders are typically great listeners. Informal interactions where you might pose an open-ended question and then become a great listener are the fuel that develops an organization that everyone wants to be a part of. How to be a great listener and then scale that to a large organization will be covered in the next 2 chapters.

11

Listening

"Hearing is a God-given ability, but listening is a defining value."

Richard Shuman, MD

I never wanted to be a physician. I grew up in a family of dentists and dental hygienists and knew that was not going to be my career path. The idea of putting my hand in people's mouths for a career was a non-starter.

When I was in 5th and 6th grade, I liked the idea of acting. I tried out for the school play but was not chosen for the role. I tried out for several other plays in 7th and 8th grade. Once again, I came close but never made the cut. Unfortunately, at the age of 13, I let a drama teacher's opinion deter me from continuing to pursue my interest in acting.

When I was 15, I transferred to an all-boys day private school in Massachusetts. It turned out to be the best decision in my young life, one that was made for me. Seeing how unhappy I was in public school, my mother picked me up early one day and took me to a private school she thought might be a better fit. The academic year had started about a month prior, but she was not concerned. She insisted that I could catch up, and before I knew it, I was attending a new school with fifty other 15-year-old boys.

In 9th grade, I had the great fortune of having an amazing biology class with Pierre Latour. The material was interesting, and it made sense to me. In addition, Mr. Latour was vibrant and excited about the material. I was hooked, and for the first time, started to do well academically. Pierre believed in me, and I began to believe in myself. Thinking back to this time in my life, I am reminded of the importance of positive feedback and having someone who believes in you.

I decided to pursue the sciences, but I was still drawn to the humanities. I especially loved art and art history. During my senior year, a course on art history was taught by Jack Jarzeveck. It was iconic; we would sit in a dark room as Jack commandeered the slide projector to show art from around the world. I remember feeling like I was traveling in time, connecting with Vermeer, Rembrandt, and all the other 17th-century Dutch masters. It was a life-changing experience. I considered pursuing a career as an artist or museum curator. Unfortunately, neither of these jobs paid very well and was not well regarded by my parents. I remember thinking to myself, if I wasn't going to pursue art, what was I going to do? What was I good at?

I remember in my senior year of high school sitting with Pierre who by that point was a close friend. He was having a tough day, and I could tell he wasn't himself. I earnestly asked him, "Is there anything I can do to make your day better?" He smiled and laughed, likely finding it ironic that someone so young would ask such a question. He paused for a long time and then said something that has stayed with me to this day: "Sometimes just acknowledging someone's pain is enough". He followed by saying: "You are a great kid and an even better listener. Make sure you find a career path that allows you to use this special talent."

His words penetrated my psyche, and I began to believe that I was a great listener. As a result, I began working, even as a young adult, on becoming even better at this. When it came time to choose a career, I asked myself what could be more meaningful than becoming a physician? Such a career could balance my interest in science with my ability to listen. At the time, I also envisioned a side hustle as an artist.

Over time, I have found that being an attentive listener is the most valuable tool a physician can have. You might think having clinical knowledge or great technical skill would be more important, but that is not true. I have heard some internal medicine physicians state that forty percent of their clinical practice is related to the management of depression or anxiety. People tend not to walk into a physician's office and say, "I am depressed." Instead, they arrive with symptoms: chest pain, shortness of breath, or abdominal pain. If you don't listen closely, you will never hear the underlying truth; their symptoms are psychological, and the pain they are experiencing is a manifestation of their sadness or anxiety.

Listening is equally important as an organizational leader. When I ask people if they are good listeners, they routinely respond in the affirmative. Ironically, they often make this comment as they are quickly glancing at their phone or their computer. Most people are good at talking and awful at listening. Even people who consider themselves to be "quiet" or "introverted" are not necessarily good listeners. The good news is that this is a skill that can be learned and improved. You may struggle to see the direct connection between listening and building a robust organizational culture. Just as the best physicians are exceptional listeners, so too are the most effective leaders. If you take the time to build your listening skills, you will not only find more joy in your job, but you will also find that others will emulate your behavior.

Several years ago, I led a course for physicians on how to build meaningful patient connections while using a computer during the visit. One of the exercises asked the providers to provide a new cancer diagnosis. (In this scenario, a colleague acted as the patient.) It was eye-opening to experience the range of provider expertise during this exercise. As I have noted previously, most cancer diagnoses are conveyed by primary care providers, so it was extremely challenging for some of the specialists to provide this type of news. Even more interesting was the level of discomfort providers experienced in sharing bad news and then transitioning to the role of active listener. The exercise was never meant to teach providers how to deliver bad news; it was meant to teach them how to be good listeners in challenging circumstances.

Since you are unlikely to be asked to perform this exercise, I will share the key takeaways from this scenario and then extrapolate them to other situations. It turns out that the best performers in this exercise did the following:

1. They informed their staff that they were about to do something challenging and that they should not be disturbed unless it was a major emergency.
2. They took the computer screen, which was on a movable stand, and pushed it to the corner of the room.
3. They had the patient sit in a chair, rather than the exam table, and pulled up a chair next to them, so they were on the same eye level.
4. They made sure that their shoulders were parallel to the patient's shoulders, so they were looking directly at each other.
5. When the patient spoke, they did not interrupt. (It is common for busy providers to interrupt patients frequently.)

6. From time to time, they would summarize what the patient said to confirm their understanding.
7. The provider strove to remain aware of nonverbal cues.
8. The provider spoke slowly, clearly, and with compassion and empathy.
9. The provider completely focused on every word the patient said, providing a sense that nothing could distract them. The patient was, for that moment, the most important person in the provider's world.

Although it was initially difficult to get providers to buy into acting out this scenario, ultimately, they did engage. By the end of the training, they had clearly improved and were better listeners for their patients.

Interestingly, the same concepts that made these providers better listeners would make you a better leader. Before I get into the details, I would emphasize the most essential aspect of active listening: attitude. You must want to listen. If you are listening but aren't interested, that will become obvious to everyone else. Poor listening, real or perceived, can quietly unravel even the strongest culture. The word will get out that you asked for people's opinions, but you really aren't interested. The opposite is equally true: a leader who meaningfully listens will create a culture where people will say, "Can you believe the CEO actually wanted my opinion and really listened to what I had to say?" When your team feels this way about you and your leadership, that's your cue to drop the mic - you've accomplished something remarkable. Here are my top suggestions for becoming a better listener:

1. Eliminate distractions: Put your phone away, step away from your computer, close your laptop, shut your door. Whatever it takes to make it clear to the

person you are talking to that you are not planning on being distracted.

2. Sit next to them: The idea of talking across a desk is not conducive to a meaningful conversation. Sit next to them with your shoulders turned towards them.
3. Sit at eye level: Make sure your chairs are at the same height. You never want to be looking down on someone.
4. Start with an act of kindness: Offer a cup of coffee, tea or water.
5. Listen with passion: Truly engage with your conversation and don't get distracted.
6. DO NOT INTERRUPT: A study showed that physicians tend to interrupt patients within 16 seconds of asking the question "What brings you in today"? Don't be like a physician. Sit on your hands if you must...but do not interrupt.
7. Be comfortable with silence: It is ok to experience silence. Do not feel the need to speak. Wait longer.
8. Watch for nonverbal cues: if people are uncomfortable, they may fidget or look away. Take these moments to be reassuring and listen more intently.
9. Did I mention that you should not interrupt.
10. Be curious. Ask follow-up questions and really try to have a deep understanding of what is being shared with you.
11. Summarize for understanding: Periodically restate what you have heard so you are both on the same page.
12. Reliable follow up: The best way for people to know that you have listened and heard them is to define clear next steps and then to live up to your commitment to follow up. This is often the most difficult part but, in my opinion, the most important.

My last point on this subject comes from one of my mentors, Dr. Joseph Kelly. He was the medical director at one of my first jobs. I remember walking into his office one day, upset about something, though it's been so long, I honestly can't recall what felt so urgent at the time. His door was open, but he was clearly working on something important. I interrupted his chain of thought and said that I needed to talk with him. He looked at me and said, "I am glad to talk with you briefly now, but you will not have my full attention. If you want my full attention, we should set up a time to talk later today or tomorrow." True listening is a meaningful endeavor and requires effort. As a leader, you are not always going to be in an emotional or physical state to be a good listener. Take the opportunity to be honest and humble with your colleagues. They will respect you more and come to understand how important it is to get your full attention.

12

Culture in a Large Organization

"Leading a large organization is not about controlling every detail; it is about creating systems, culture, and alignment that allow thousands of people to act effectively toward a common purpose."

Doris Kearns Goodwin

For most of my career, I had the good fortune to work in an organization with fewer than 200 providers. When you added the staff, the total number of employees was a little over 500. I wouldn't consider this a small organization, but with a little effort, I got to know all the providers personally and, for the most part, all the staff. Since I have always considered myself a relationship-driven leader, I enjoyed working in a slightly smaller organization.

Early in my leadership journey, I did not rely on the senior team to set the organizational culture. I felt that I alone could build relationships with everyone and imbue the organization with a clear, consistent vision and guiding principles. The key advantage of this approach was that the message was consistent: it came from one person. The downside of this approach was that the culture would not exist past the tenure of that one person, i.e., me. A culture that depends on a single person is doomed to fail.

Somewhere along the line, I realized my approach to building culture was flawed. It was time to build a team of leaders who were aligned, connected, empowered, motivated, and dedicated to the organization's mission, vision, and guiding principles. It all sounded so simple- just gather the team, offer a bit of coaching, and voilà: a thriving organizational culture. I could not have been more wrong!

I remember the first meeting I had with the leaders of each clinical department. About twelve leaders were present and, for reasons that were not clear to me at the time, they had never worked together as a team. We took a little time to introduce ourselves and began discussing the purpose and cadence of the meeting. We had planned to review key organizational issues, discuss departmental challenges, provide leadership training, and role-play complex challenges. It was an ambitious undertaking, and I initially scheduled only four two-hour meetings per year.

During the first meeting, we talked about how to have a critical conversation. This is a conversation which typically involves high stakes, differing opinions, strong emotions and impactful outcomes. We even role-played a real discussion that one of the department chiefs was preparing to have in the coming days. It was an amazing moment! A group of people who did not know each other well came together to support one of their colleagues, sharing both positive feedback and thoughtful criticism. A palpable camaraderie emanated from that first two-hour session. Nobody wanted it to end.

As I do at the end of all meetings, participants were asked to give positive feedback on the meeting and then share what they would change. This concept is referred to as a "plus-delta". It forces participants to provide a balanced evaluation of the meeting and promotes important discussion around how to improve the meeting going forward. Given that this was the initial meeting, I asked the group whether they thought it was a good use of their time and whether we should continue meeting. Their responses shocked me; they asked for the meetings to go longer and to meet more frequently. Ultimately, this group met for four-hour sessions every month.

Over time, this team began to develop trust in one another. They actively supported each other and, most importantly, began to take ownership and be accountable. At first, they were very reluctant to embrace their positional authority and lead their departments. Ultimately, however, they developed a tremendous feeling of pride not just in their departments, but for the entire organization. They started to understand and develop comfort with how decisions were made in the organization, and this process aligned with their values.

It wasn't that complicated. Every month for four hours, we would share our challenges, support each other, and live our values. Interestingly, we never wrote down our guiding principles, but we all knew it boiled down to a straightforward concept: "Do the Right Thing".

As the CEO, I was always available to the senior leaders, and at first, they had many questions. They needed both emotional support and basic leadership education. Over time, that need for direct support abated. I often heard people ask, "What would Rich do?", usually followed by the confident answer, "He'd want me to just Do the Right Thing." They were correct—I would support any of their actions if they came from the right place and they were trying to Do the Right Thing.

It is important to note that to Do the Right Thing in a large organization is often difficult. Situations are gray, and decision-making can be very challenging. It is easy to overlook bad behavior and to choose conflict avoidance over organizational consistency. These leaders were not perfect, but they worked hard to live their values and were genuinely committed to creating an organization they were proud to be part of, both as leaders and as caregivers.

You may be wondering how this translates into the creation of culture within a large organization. The truth is that, as a CEO, it can be difficult to be a relationship-driven leader. There is no way you can have a personal relationship with 2000 providers and 10,000 staff. For years, I have struggled with how someone with a leadership style like mine could lead a larger entity.

I have had the opportunity to work, albeit not as a CEO, in two very large organizations. The details of these positions are not particularly important, but what is notable is the one key similarity between the two roles: inconsistent middle management. When you sit in the C-suite, it is common to see aligned mission, vision, and values. If you are lucky, you can build an experienced and high performing senior leadership team. If you are exceptionally fortunate, you can create a team with similar leadership values and accountability expectations to those you hold as a CEO. The question is whether those senior leaders disseminate that culture to the teams that they build.

This is where the difference between a small organization and a large organization becomes clearly apparent. In a small organization, the senior leadership team serves as the direct link between the CEO and frontline employees. In a larger organization, there are likely at least one (and possibly two) additional layers of management. In both large organizations where I worked, there was a clear disconnect between the CEO/senior leaders and the managers/supervisors. Since managers/supervisors were in direct contact with the front line, the cultural vision's movement failed to cascade to the entire organization.

Most CEOs of organizations focus on senior leadership. The belief is that if you provide the senior leaders with education, leadership training, and organizational values, then you will be able to build the culture you are looking for. I think this approach is necessary but not sufficient.

As a CEO, you need to get more involved with the lower level of leadership, the directors and managers. They need to understand that the organization's values are more than just a piece of paper, that you care about them as people, and that we are all working to build a culture of kindness and respect. They need to understand that they must be accountable and that you will have their back if they meaningfully try to do the right thing.

Historically, providing performance feedback between a senior leader and leaders who were not their direct reports was frowned upon. It created a level of angst from the senior leaders and made them feel like they were being micromanaged and not doing their job adequately. In the past, I accepted that rationale and avoided such interactions. That was a mistake. I am not suggesting that you micromanage employees or managers who are several layers below you in the organizational chart, but I am suggesting that they need to see you and get to know you. They need to relate to you as a person and a leader. That does not happen through large group meetings. Personal connection is essential to creating a consistent cultural message.

I don't want to oversimplify the building of organizational culture in a large business. However, I do believe in the "One Thing" principle as defined by Gary Keller in his best-selling book of the same name. Simply put, Keller notes that if you focus on the one most important task, everything else will become easier or unnecessary. In this case, the most important task is for the CEO to take the time to connect with leaders at all levels in their organization. This is a lot of work and time to invest, but it's worth it when everyone feels proud to live the organization's meaningful values.

It is tempting to end the chapter here, but I feel an additional story would help reinforce my point. When I was the medical director of an organization with about 500 staff members, I made a concerted effort to connect with middle management and, given the organization's manageable size, I knew most of the frontline staff. This group had many risk-based contracts and, as a result, quality performance was essential to financial success.

To maximize our performance, the senior leaders and front-line managers would meet frequently to discuss our quality performance and care gaps. We called this group "Quality by Design". As we looked at our performance scorecard, it was obvious to everyone that we were failing to get children between birth and 15 months to come in for their scheduled appointments and immunizations. We had endless discussions on why we were failing to meet this goal, and we tried multiple interventions. The result of these interventions was no improvement at all.

One day, I was visiting one of the clinical sites, and the front desk person smiled at me and said, "Dr Shuman, can I talk to you for a moment?" I walked into her workspace and said, "Sure, what can I help you with?" She responded, "I know why we are not meeting the pediatric visit and immunization goal." I must admit that I was extremely skeptical, given that the leadership had been working on this for many months, albeit unsuccessfully. However, I was really pleased that she knew and had been thinking about the organizational goals. I also wondered at that moment why, if she did have the answer to this important issue, she didn't share it with her manager. I then realized that her manager was not very strong and had not bought into our organizational culture. In addition, the manager was quite gruff and difficult to approach.

I responded, "That sounds great. What do you think the problem is?" She responded, "When pediatric patients don't come to their appointments, we do not put them on the reschedule list. We only do that for patients who cancel appointments."

I wondered if this was just a process failure for this clinical office rather than an organizational issue. I wondered if this was a PICNIC (Problem In Chair Not In Computer). That said, I knew the no-show rate for Pediatrics was around 8-10 percent and that this would account for our care gap.

At the next day's leadership meeting, I brought forward the comments from the receptionist. You could have heard a pin drop. Clearly, this was the missing link. We addressed this issue and ultimately met our pediatric goal.

The moral of this story is simple. If you have built a connection with your front-line managers and staff, they are very likely to buy into the organizational values and culture. They will take the time to understand the goals and work towards meeting them. As a leader, you might initiate a strategy, but success depends on your direct reports and front-line staff. Being able to connect and meaningfully communicate with your middle management is important in small organizations and essential in large ones.

13

An Executive Coach

"A coach is someone who sees the talent in you that you may not see yourself and helps you grow it. Leaders who are willing to listen to coaching are the ones who continue to grow."

John C. Maxwell

I was a practicing physician for a little over 30 years, and my profession changed significantly over that time. There were incredible advancements and extreme challenges, but what did not change was the need for clinicians who could assess, diagnose, and treat patients. An individual came to you with a set of concerns and complaints, often combined with uncertainty, fear, and anxiety, and you had to assess the situation, formulate a reasonable differential diagnosis, and start a treatment regimen.

For care providers, this is all routine and core to their everyday activities. However, there is one key underlying skill that all providers must come to grips with: dealing with uncertainty. The untold secret of healthcare is that we often really don't know what the problem is. It can be a little disconcerting at first. Still, you quickly learn to accept that, except for strep throat and maybe earwax blocking the ear canal, we often are just dealing with relative probabilities of what might be the issue with any patient. Almost all physicians need to build confidence in dealing with uncertainty.

The ability to deal with uncertainty permeates every day of a physician's work life. This shield of confidence related to uncertainty allows you to manage expansive expectations of patients and their families. It allows you to get through your day and to sleep at night. In some cases, however, this confidence can lead to physician arrogance. Such arrogance can make it challenging to be an organizational leader. An overconfidence in your abilities can also result in extrapolating your clinical skills to every other aspect of your life. The thinking often goes: if I'm a good physician, I must also be a solid financial investor, an effective leader, and even a skilled chef. Those who feel like gods in a medical environment may have little tolerance for not feeling that way in other parts of their lives. In boardrooms and executive positions, this is a liability, and I have found that physicians are often not the exceptional leaders they believe themselves to be.

A combination of physician arrogance and refusal to see leadership as a separate skill set creates a resistance to accepting help. Physician leaders might attend a few courses on leadership, usually required by the organization, but they are unlikely to accept meaningful one-on-one help on a routine basis. This is a costly mistake.

Undervaluing the importance of coaching is one of the core oversights of large organizations. As I mentioned in the previous chapter, connecting senior leadership with middle management is essential to success in a large organization. One of the best ways to connect is to invest in their development and leadership skills. Understanding how to be a leader will allow them to better receive the messages they are receiving from their bosses and develop the necessary tools to convey that message effectively to their direct reports. Investing in executive coaching — not just for the CEO and senior leaders but also for middle management — may be one of the most impactful decisions an organization can make. Unfortunately, it is rare for an organization to make this kind of investment.

I met my future executive coach, Gina Ohanesian, MSOB, at a group training session over 15 years ago. At the time, she was providing group training through an employment association, and I was the Chief of Medicine at my medical group. It was outstanding training because, unlike the other seminars, she allowed the group to guide the discussion. We covered meeting management, public speaking, and listening skills, and she demonstrated a truly impressive level of expertise wherever the discussion went. I approached her after the meeting, shared my positive feedback, and asked her to help with additional training at my organization. Thus began a long relationship that evolved from group training to her serving as my own executive coach.

Gina taught me how to be a leader—from the fundamentals of running meetings and developing presentations to crafting guiding principles and mission statements, and ultimately to becoming an effective leader who builds strong organizational culture. I was, admittedly, one of those physicians who came with a level of overconfidence and thought, at times, that I just knew better. In retrospect, I didn't. However, I did embrace the reason I became a doctor: I was a good listener. I listened intently to my executive coach's ideas. I wrote them down and I did what any good doctor would do: I tested out the hypotheses. Gina would provide me with ideas, and I would routinely implement them. I allowed myself to be a student. I encouraged myself to be humble and to value the input of a subject-matter expert. It wasn't always easy, but I knew that I wanted to be a great leader and that I needed help to accomplish that goal.

One day, I was meeting with Gina, and she looked at me and said, "You are the best student I have ever mentored". I greatly valued that feedback and pushed my ego aside to appreciate and embrace the role of student. Yes, I had gone through medical school, residency, and decades of clinical practice, but there was always more to learn. I share this anecdote not to pat myself on the back, but because, if you are going to invest in an executive coach, you must accept that you are not a subject-matter expert and you must embrace being the student, even if you have been the mentor to others for decades.

The notion of being an executive coach to middle management is compelling. In some ways, writing this book is a way to share some of my ideas in this arena. However, I come back to a point that I made earlier in this chapter: there is a distinct difference between concepts of leadership and the daily challenges of being a leader. An executive coach helps you balance general knowledge with daily work. It also allows someone to speak truth to power, which direct reports are often reluctant to do.

14

Ear Wax: Dealing with Uncertainty

"Personal courage, often lonely courage, is essential for a great leader because everyone else below has passed the buck."

Father John Cavanaugh

I've always tried to "Do the Right Thing", and I often find myself asking, "Am I doing the right thing?"—both in my personal life and in my career. Unfortunately, despite being a simple question, life is rarely black or white. As previously noted, dealing with uncertainty is an important skill to develop.

I had the good fortune to attend the University of Massachusetts Medical School. During those 4 years, I dissected a human cadaver, learned about normal human physiology, and learned about human diseases and the body's response to them. Although it was a monumental amount of information gained through endless days and nights of studying, I have never been so engaged in learning. I remember, upon graduation, feeling that I possessed potent knowledge.

At the time, there were no cellphones and, for the most part, no personal computers. All knowledge resided in books and libraries. It was essential that physicians, young and old, had an excellent understanding of medicine, since the resources for consultation were much more limited than they are today.

After I finished medical school, I continued my training at Dartmouth Hitchcock Medical Center. This stage, residency, is so named because young doctors spend so much time in the hospital that they are essentially in residence there. Dartmouth Medical Center, which sits in picturesque Lebanon, New Hampshire, was the first place where I was given the terrifying responsibility of caring for patients.

For a physician, it is impossible to forget the first day of residency. First-year residents are called interns. They are easy to spot because, at least back in 1990, they wore short white coats, a specific color of scrubs (fancy pajamas), and were very excited to be wearing their very first electronic pager, fondly referred to as "a beeper". For reasons that I can't quite explain, I did not wear my short white coat on my first day of internship. I wore a pink button-down shirt, a pale blue vest, and khaki pants. I think I was either in denial, or I wasn't comfortable with identifying as a doctor. After all, I still considered myself a failed art museum curator.

On my first rotation, I cared for cancer patients as well as patients undergoing bone marrow transplants. There was a special section of the hospital for these very ill, immunocompromised patients, and I was both excited and nervous to be "on the inside" taking care of these individuals. I was assigned to one patient receiving a bone marrow transplant, and I spent a considerable amount of time reviewing the chart, speaking with the patient, examining him, and, for the first time, writing an order in the chart.

Although I can't remember my first order, I imagine it was something incredibly benign, like "Tylenol 500 mg 1-2 tablets by mouth every 8 hours as needed for pain or fever". At the time, it felt like a monumental achievement. Somehow, I had trained long enough and performed well enough that I was now trusted to provide a course of treatment, and nurses, pharmacists, and other doctors with more experience than I had years on this Earth would listen to me. It doesn't sound quite so exciting when my initial order was for a medication you could get at CVS, but you get the idea.

Later that first day, my beeper buzzed in my pocket. I eagerly looked at it and saw a number pop up on the screen. Excitedly, I walked to the nearest hospital phone (this was before cellphones) and called the number. On the other end of the line was the person who would one day become my wife – though I couldn't have known it then. She calmly informed me that our mutual bone marrow transplant patient had developed a fever and wanted to ask if I wanted to do anything about it.

I knew that I was supposed to know the answer to her question, but I was uncertain about the best course of action. I paused on the phone for what seemed like an eternity. Knowing it was my first day on the job and sensing my uncertainty, Elinor Gilleran, RN decided to provide a long list of suggestions. Unsurprisingly, those were exactly the right steps to take. Massively relieved, I replied, "That sounds great".

My purpose in retelling this story is not to share the challenges of internship or even to remind everyone what an amazing and compassionate nurse my wife was and is (although that is probably a good enough reason on its own). It is not even to tell you that I met my wife on my first day of residency and that she noticed me because I was confident enough to wear a pink shirt and a pale blue sweater vest. The point of the story is that, on the very first day of residency, I experienced a tremendously uncomfortable feeling of uncertainty. It was a paralyzing fear that I did not know what to do and that I might do the wrong thing.

Later during that first week of residency, I was on call, which is a gentle way of saying the new guy had to stay at the hospital for a 36-hour shift. I would assist with all new hospital admissions, take care of currently admitted patients, and support any Code Blues. A Code Blue is a hospital term for a patient who is in extreme peril. It often means that the patient has either stopped breathing or that their heart has stopped working. As a member of the Code Blue team, when your beeper went off, you sprinted to the patient's side and did your best to resuscitate them.

To say that I was nervous during my first on-call night is the understatement of the century. I felt reasonably comfortable admitting and taking care of patients because, by then, I had done it for a few days. The idea of helping on a Code Blue, however, made me nauseous. I was hoping that my first night would be uneventful, and no one would require resuscitation.

Around 3:00 am, however, a Code Blue notification appeared on my beeper. I jumped from my on-call room's bed. I was sleepy but had been unable to fall asleep. I dashed across the hospital to the patient's room. The nurse was already there, so I was the second person to arrive.

The fear I felt at that very moment was overwhelming. I had trained to help in Code Blue situations, but there is a big difference between training on a mannequin and seeing a real person who is pulseless and lying motionless on a hospital bed. For the second time in less than a week, I was riddled with uncertainty. What should I do? I want to help. I want to do the right thing. But what if I do the wrong thing?

Although it seemed like an eternity, several other Code Blue team members joined us moments later. The most experienced resident took charge and instructed me to do chest compressions. I gladly complied with the request and pushed on the elderly patient's chest. I recall thinking that I had performed chest compressions on a mannequin before and that this task, which required only repetitive action and minimal critical thinking, should be no problem. I stood on a stool above the patient's chest and began my first chest compression. The patient, unlike the mannequin, had ribs that gave way under the pressure of my compressions. I realized that I had broken several of his ribs and momentarily froze. The senior resident told me to continue compressions, so I did. Less than 30 minutes later, the patient was pronounced dead. The resident called it just like on TV: "Time of death: 3:48 AM."

After the Code Blue, the senior resident pulled me aside and asked if I was ok. He saw that I had broken the patients' ribs and was also aware this has been my first Code Blue. To appear tough, I responded, "I am fine." He paused and said, "It is ok not to be fine. I have run lots of codes, but they are still difficult. I always wonder if I should have done something different that might have made a difference."

I didn't realize it at the time, but, in retrospect, the senior resident was struggling with uncertainty as well. He was desperately trying to save someone's life, but despite doing everything he thought possible, he lived with doubt.

As a primary care physician, I would typically see 20 to 25 patients per day. Some of these visits were routine follow-ups, but many were acute problems. I know that this is going to be uncomfortable for many non-medical people reading this book, but most of the time, physicians are not sure what is wrong with you. In fact, we are trained to come up with a range of possible diagnoses since it is so common that we don't initially know the actual diagnosis. We are trained that we will not always know the correct answer and that uncertainty is the norm.

I recall early in my career thinking that there were only two diagnoses that I was certain of. The first was Strep throat. This was a straightforward diagnosis, as the patient presented with a severe sore throat, and we had a rapid test that would yield a positive result in the office. You could call it "certainty in a box".

The other diagnosis I loved was blocked ears due to wax. I would flush someone's ears with warm water, dislodge the wax, and miraculously restore one of their five senses. Why work through uncertainty when I could spend my career definitively fixing simple problems? It is comforting for physicians to practice evidence-based medicine but, if we are being honest, there is not much clarity when dealing with the complexities of patient illness.

I would argue that the most important lesson I learned as a physician is not how to properly diagnose an illness, but to identify whether a patient is merely sick or, in contrast, truly ill. I know this seems like a distinction without a difference, but it is likely the most important decision a clinician can make.

Patients whom I would call "sick" tended to have a benign self-limited illness, while patients who were "ill" needed intervention and sometimes even hospitalization. One of my colleagues once said, "It is our job to identify the people who are going to die if we don't do something. Everyone else will call back."

I realize this is a lighthearted way of looking at medical care, but being able to discern sick from ill is an essential clinical skill. It also reinforces that good physicians have experience in discerning illness and dealing with the uncertainty of not knowing the answer. Excellent physicians make the best decisions they can with the information available to them at the time. Nothing more, nothing less.

Just as medical training equips physicians to navigate uncertainty, it can also help them feel at ease in organizational leadership, a role equally steeped in ambiguity. Great leadership means embracing uncertainty while striving to make the right decisions, choices that may shape the lives of thousands of employees and customers for years to come.

As a CEO, you are often surrounded by subject matter experts offering guidance on both what should be done and how to do it. Among the most frequent sources of input is the senior leadership team—a group typically composed of hard-working, talented, and deeply invested individuals who genuinely want the organization to succeed. Their advice is usually well intentioned and shaped by their perspectives and experiences, with the shared goal of helping the organization move forward successfully. Usually, there is only one problem: they have never been CEO. This is not to say they have not overseen their piece of the organization. This is also not to say that they do not care about doing the right thing. It is to say they have not experienced the weight of being a CEO. Since it is often unclear how to "Do the Right Thing", the weight of this uncertainty lies on the shoulders of the CEO, as does ultimate accountability.

As an organizational leader, you must accept that uncertainty. For some leaders, this seems easy and almost seamless. For the best leaders, building an organizational culture that they and their employees are proud of is a daily struggle. Your willingness to struggle shows that you care, and it is this struggle that makes you a great leader in a great organization.

I want to end this discussion with advice that I give to other leaders, to my children, and often to myself: embrace the difficult question of doing what is right. Struggle with your decisions and get input from those whom you trust. Make the best decision you can with the information you have at that moment. Do your best to accept that your decision will ultimately be yours alone.

15

Fake it 'til you make it

"You succeed because you've chosen to be confident. It's not really useful to require yourself to be successful before you're able to become confident."

Seth Godin

It is important to be transparent about the nature of leadership. The idea that people are born leaders is simply unrealistic. Individuals may have some innate characteristics that predispose them to being a good leader, but those need to be combined with experience and training to develop into meaningful leadership. The truth is that most leaders, if they are honest, enter the role with a tremendous amount of doubt and uncertainty. Some leaders, especially those with more dominant personality types, may hide that uncertainty better than others, but everyone experiences it.

When I was first put in charge of a moderate size private medical practice, I struggled with being a leader. I was very young, did not have any real leadership experience, and was asked to lead the group primarily because no one else was interested. I will never forget my early efforts at running department meetings. I tried to bring some consistency and standardization, but the other physicians were not interested in hearing from a young, precocious Doogie Houser. (I know I'm dating myself again with TV references, but, trust me, this is funny.) I was frequently ignored, and physicians often did not come to the meetings. I was periodically ridiculed for my lack of experience and denigrated for my religious affiliation. Apparently, it was bad enough to be led by someone young, but it was somehow worse still to be led by someone young and Jewish. I struggled to find my footing and wanted to walk away from the leadership role and return to what I had been trained to do: take care of patients.

I wish I could tell you that I had an epiphany and developed an elegant way to deal with my detractors, that those individuals quickly learned to embrace my leadership style and saw the light, and that leadership was my destiny. Unfortunately, none of that is true. I stayed in the job because I had a young family, and I wanted the extra money to provide opportunities for my wife and children. Given that personal choice, I needed to develop a strategy to deal with a group of physicians who clearly did not respect me or value my leadership.

I started by finding a group of doctors who had bought into my vision, which focused on doing the right thing and prioritizing the needs of patients over those of providers. I realized that, to create a true tipping point in the organization, I needed to recruit enough physicians who shared this mindset, making any other approach uncomfortable. This change took time and effort. I had to work one-on-one with early adopters and hire only people who fit the new mold. This is the hard work of organizational culture change. A consistent approach is required to obtain the change you want. Anyone who tells you differently is just lying to you to make you feel better about your leadership and organization.

After about four years in my new leadership role, I could feel the momentum of the organization changing. In meetings, the physicians who were resistors were confronted by the early adopters. I was no longer the only one standing up for our new vision and values. The staff bought in and knew that, if they did the right thing, they would be supported by leadership. As the saying goes, "change happens at the speed of trust"; the organization was starting to trust the leaders.

It was at this point that I made another questionable strategic decision. I knew the culture of the organization was changing, but I also knew that the staff and the physicians had to believe that they were part of something special. For employees to connect to an organization, they need to feel valued, respected, and part of something bigger than themselves. I had taken for granted the last aspect of this connection. I had assumed that working in the revered healing arts would provide its own sense of greater purpose. I learned, however, that a sense of pride and connection occurs only if you believe you are providing a high level of care. If you are constantly dealing with medical errors and apologizing for behavioral issues, you are not going to feel connected to a higher purpose. Once I came to this understanding, I knew I had to create the organizational pride that was sorely lacking.

As it turns out, there is a lag between organizational cultural change and clinical outcomes. As a leader, I could sense the change, but waiting for the outcomes was incredibly frustrating. It was at this point that I realized we had to "fake it till we made it". I made a conscious decision to provide positive feedback to the group despite not having any objective data. At group meetings, I would frequently say, "You are some of the highest quality physicians in the state." I might add, "This group is setting the standard for care in Western

Massachusetts." Neither of those statements was true. Historically, the group had poor clinical performance and, by all objective metrics, was just average.

However, by this point in our cultural journey, they had come to trust me and the leadership. If I shared with them that they were amazing, they were likely to believe it. In fact, even the resistors began to believe that they were part of an outstanding clinical group. Perhaps to no one's surprise, their belief resulted in significantly improved performance. They were more open to process changes and embraced both personal and professional standards. Soon afterwards, the clinical outcomes improved, and we really did become one of the best medical groups in the state.

Looking back, I am not overly proud of my dishonesty. I am not going to try to justify it, and perhaps now I would take a different approach. In any event, it is important to note that taking pride in your work and your organization is essential to a strong organizational culture, robust employee engagement, and strong business outcomes. We all need to feel like our work is making a difference. As a leader, it is essential to ensure that, no matter your business, you create an environment where everyone feels they are valued, respected, and part of something bigger.

It reminds me of the story about someone asking a NASA janitor what his job was. He replied, "My job is to help land a man on the moon." That connection to the greater mission is what takes good organizations and makes them great!

16

The Weight of Leadership

"Nearly all men can stand adversity, but if you want to test a man's character, give him power."

Abraham Lincoln

This chapter was written several years ago, but it remains in the present tense by design. The immediacy of that voice best conveys the angst of the moment.

I recently turned 60 and have been a physician leader for almost 30 years. As I am writing this, it is 3:42 in the morning, and I can't sleep. I had a difficult meeting with my board of directors yesterday, and I am struggling to let it go. As I lay in bed trying to convince myself to go back to sleep, I realized it was the perfect opportunity to discuss an aspect of leadership that is rarely recognized: the weight of being a good leader.

Many have heard the phrase "It's lonely at the top," but that saying oversimplifies a deeper, often-overlooked reality: the unique and underappreciated challenges faced by organizational leaders. It is essential to take a moment to consider this from a personal perspective as well as how it affects organizational culture.

One of my colleagues recently expressed interest in becoming a CEO. He is a fantastic person and an excellent leader. He approached me and asked what the most challenging part of being a CEO is. I hadn't thought much about this topic and told him I needed to reflect on it and that I would get back to him.

Later, I took some time to think about the challenges of being a CEO. Many resources examine the characteristics of great leaders; experts highlight resilience, emotional intelligence, and a balanced personality profile. I agree with all those traits but would also include the ability to deal with the weight of leadership.

The weight of leadership is difficult to describe. Words like "accountability" or "responsibility" don't aptly describe the feeling an engaged CEO will experience in their role. The best way I can describe it is by sharing what it is not. It is not the feeling of personal responsibility, like when you must give a presentation or complete a work assignment. It is not the feeling of making an error, like when you provide an incorrect financial analysis. It is not the feeling of making a difficult decision, like when you must choose who to hire and who to fire.

It is perhaps a sense of wanting to do the right thing, not knowing exactly what the right thing is, but knowing you are totally responsible for its results. It is a demand for you to provide certainty when there is none, to decide and carry the weight of that decision while others question its validity.

When the decision turns out to be a good one, great leaders share the credit. In fact, it is common to forget that it was even a difficult decision in the first place. Bad decisions, however, fall directly at your feet. You must own them and live with the negativity and second-guessing that always comes, both from within and from others. Every leader understands the quiet weight of responsibility – the early mornings staring at the walls, wrestling with decisions, and secretly longing for the day when the journey ends and the invisible burden of leadership is finally lifted.

Another leadership challenge was one I did not fully appreciate until later in my career. It started when I was asked by my director to terminate several leaders because of significant financial pressures facing the organization. These individuals were highly respected and effective in their roles, and I struggled with the request. I believed there might be alternatives that would address the financial realities without losing such strong leadership, and I worked hard to explore other options. My director was understandably focused on the organization's financial health, and any alternative would need to meet those same fiscal requirements. After a restless night, I developed a proposal that consolidated additional responsibilities under these leaders while eliminating several unfilled leadership positions.

The next morning, I went to present the idea. As I waited outside the office, I felt physically drained and deeply uneasy. I remember thinking that I would have been more comfortable responding to a Code Blue than having that conversation. When the door opened, I was shown into the office. I was asked directly whether I had carried out the terminations that were requested. I answered, more hesitantly than I would have liked, "No." I then walked him through my alternative plan, explaining how it would address the financial concerns while retaining experienced leadership. After a long pause my boss said, "I'm comfortable with your plan, but if it doesn't work, we may need to think about alternative financial consolidations." Although he never specifically said so, it was clear, in my mind, that the consolidation was me.

After this difficult episode, I realized it was time to find a different employer and reflected on how close I had come to making a decision that could have harmed outstanding leaders I considered friends. Could I balance between being friends with my employees and maintaining just enough space to be their boss? This is a difficult tightrope act. The phrase "It is lonely at the top" reflects more than just the burden of tough decisions; it also speaks to the isolation that comes from having colleagues at work but few truly close relationships there.

Here is another story concerning how leadership can be isolating. One day when I was still working my clinical job, I asked my office nurse Melanie to lunch. I honestly did not think twice about it. I was hungry, there was a pizza shop next door to the office, and I didn't want to eat another lunch alone behind my desk. Melanie graciously accepted and we walked to the pizza joint. After we ordered, we sat down at a table and waited for our food. The pizza shop was very popular, so I didn't think twice that employees from the group came in to pick up their orders.

Melanie and I had a lovely lunch and returned to the office to return to our work. Later that day, Melanie was approached by several other staff members inquiring about the nature of her lunch with me. They shared with her their concerns that she was getting "favorable" treatment since Melanie and I were friends. I remember feeling shocked that having lunch with an employee would garner that type of attention and angry that I had to consider what other people might think when I made my lunch plans.

The entire incident reminded me how difficult it was as a CEO to have close friends at work. It reinforced for me that CEOs need to accept the fact that everyone is watching. They observe how you speak, where you eat, and how you dress. They also note whether you treat everyone respectfully or play favorites. The CEO is the architect of corporate culture, and a failure to accept the responsibility and weight of the role can quickly erode it.

17

A Day in the Life

"A leader must understand the challenges of every player on the team. Only by walking alongside them can you truly help them excel."

John Wooden

Once I became the CEO of a medical group, I soon felt disconnected from the organization's work. I sat in meetings all day, and my clinical work dwindled immensely. I became isolated from the staff and colleagues, and work became less fun.

I asked other CEOs for advice, and they recommended that I do rounds, meeting folks in their work environment to get a sense of their challenges. Rounding, however, proved to be an unmitigated disaster. Everyone was on their best behavior, the front-line folks were too intimidated to ask meaningful questions, and I was too shy to facilitate meaningful interactions.

I quickly stopped rounding and sought an alternative. I may have been watching an episode of "Undercover Boss", a television show in which CEOs dress up as front-line employees to spy on their own organizations, when I came up with the idea of "a day in the life". I knew that my organization was too small for me to disguise myself, but I could spend time experiencing each role within the company.

With significant trepidation, I scheduled days to shadow and attempt to perform the activities of each position in the company. I want to stress that the true value of this activity wasn't in the shadowing itself, but in the effort to step into their role and attempt to do the job. I started with the role of the physician assistant. Since I had been a physician for many years, this was the easiest role for me to assume. This day turned out to be fun, and I thought that I was on to something. Acting as a check-in receptionist was next on the list.

I showed up at the front desk on a Tuesday morning. The receptionists were all very excited to see me, but their eyes held a trace of trepidation. I spent the morning shadowing them and learning what was required to check someone in for their visit. They confirmed personal information and insurance information. This was followed by obtaining additional medical information and ensuring that all the disclosures were up to date. The receptionists would also sign up patients for our patient portal and provide them with surveys. All of this was performed while maintaining reasonable eye contact and conversing with the patient. It was a fantastic balancing act. As I sat there, I realized that these employees were likely among the lowest-paid workers in our organization, yet, in many ways, they were its most visible representatives. I also started to have a feeling of dread because that afternoon, I was going to sit in their chair and check people in myself.

I ate lunch with the receptionists, who knew that my morning shadowing would soon be followed by my attempt to perform their job. They found this hilarious, but they also felt compassion for me. Most importantly, they were appreciative that the CEO was taking the time to understand their challenges.

Lunch ended quickly, and we went back to work. I tried to check-in my first patient, but it was an absolute disaster. I struggled with every aspect and didn't come close to making a connection with the patient. I was so bad that I had to step aside and let a receptionist step in. My enthusiasm was not extinguished, however, after that one massive embarrassment. That took at least five patients, a queue of patients halfway down the hallway, and a gentle request from the supervisor to let the experts do their job.

By the end of that day, I had learned just how challenging check-in work really is. I developed an appreciation for the receptionists not just as workers but as people. More importantly, I realized that the next time we discussed a project in the leadership team that added work to the check-in process, I could say with authority that assigning "just one more thing" was simply unreasonable.

Over the next several months, I tried and failed at a myriad of jobs. I found tremendous joy in my failures, and so did the workers who performed these jobs each day. The project made me seem more authentic and approachable. I was reminded that success is exciting, but failure is an equally powerful and much more relatable experience.

It also reminded me that at the heart of most people is the desire to help others. By showing vulnerability, I allowed my employees to assume the role of teacher as I played their student. This was by far the most rewarding aspect of the experience.

As a leader, you might note that this is a cute project, but one that you could never pursue in your organization. You may say that your organization is simply too big, and that you have more important things to do. To you leaders who say this, I have one response: you are wrong!

My experience at the reception desk spread like wildfire throughout the organization. The goodwill I had earned that day created a momentum that I was able to draw from for years to come. It helped drive the culture of the staff and made them feel valued and respected by leadership, not just me.

I know that we often equate financial compensation with staff feeling valued and respected. In truth, that is just one small aspect of that equation. Staff, like all people, just want to be heard and be led by someone they can relate to. If you sit in your office and they only see you through a videoconference, you will never achieve a truly great culture.

18

Work Life Balance

"Authentic leaders know that personal well-being is inseparable from professional effectiveness. Modeling balance is a signal to your organization that you care about people, not just results."

Bill George

Work-life balance is a hot topic these days. The recent pandemic heightened focus on this tenuous balance. It fostered a workforce highly interested in flexible hours and remote work, while increasing the desire to address personal needs outside the office.

As a physician who trained almost 30 years ago, the concept of work-life balance is lost on me. During my training, it was not unusual to work 100-hour weeks. Once I began private practice, my hours improved, but the idea of a work week that didn't include nights and weekends was not even a consideration. That being said, I believe that the push to create a better life balance is absolutely the right move for workers, leaders, and businesses. The question is how to promote a culture that emphasizes work outcomes while also valuing employees' personal lives. It is a difficult challenge, but one thing is certain: the culture needs to be driven by the leadership team.

Many years ago, I sat in a meeting with a new leader. As he introduced himself to his team, he noted the importance of the people in that room having work-life balance but followed that statement by noting that he "planned to be available to the organization 24/7/365". Although I am sure the comment was intended to convey his dedication to his job and to his new organization, it had a different impact than the one he intended. Unfortunately, in the eyes of his leadership team, it immediately contradicted his previous statement. Everyone assumed that, if their supervisor was going to be available every minute of every day, then the expectation was the same for his direct reports.

Another classic way a leader undermines efforts to create a culture of work-life balance is through email. Have you ever received an email from your boss in the evening or on the weekend? Did you respond? How did it make you feel? As leaders, we often find ourselves working unusual hours. An idea may come to you, and you want to share it before you forget it. You quickly compose an email and send it, not realizing it is 9:00 pm on a Friday. Your employee might get that email on their phone and feel compelled to respond. They may need to involve others to provide an adequate response. It is now too late; you have taken a first step into creating a culture that does not respect your employees' personal time.

Here's one last example that I think may be helpful. In an earlier leadership role, I reported to a director who was new to the role and had difficulty prioritizing. Everything was treated as an emergency, which created a culture of uncertainty and instability. It was commonplace for leaders to receive a text from the director, prompting them to drop everything and produce information within hours of the request.

Worse, these requests came at all times of the day and night, including weekends.

In Stephen R. Covey's classic leadership book, The 7 Habits of Highly Effective People, a graphic compares importance with urgency. At the simplest level, the graphic suggests that individuals or organizations can function in one of four quadrants: "Working on Important Things Urgently", "Working on Important Things Non-Urgently", "Working on Non-Important Things Urgently", and "Working on Non-Important Things Non-Urgently".

A leader who creates an organization that operates in the "Important but Not Urgent" quadrant produces an environment in which work is meaningful and can be accomplished within standard workdays. There is little need to send urgent texts, late-night emails, or phone calls to employees on vacation.

By adopting a non-urgent approach to work, you are more likely to achieve a work-life balance for your leaders and employees. In addition, an unanticipated emergency becomes a true rarity. Your staff is much more likely to be understanding and rally behind you. Otherwise, they may experience silent frustration with a situation that may seem like leadership's poor planning and management.

In order to build the ideal culture, you must be aware of the impact of even small comments or actions. It is often the small actions of an email, a text, a phone call, or poor planning that undermines your attempts to meet the work life balance expectations of your employees. It will always be a moving target, but being aware of the common pitfalls is a huge step in the right direction.

19

My Greatest Work Achievement

"Diversity is being invited to the party; inclusion is being asked to dance. Leaders set the rhythm."

Vernā Myers

In 1994, I took my first real job after residency. It was a large practice of primary care physicians and specialists. The primary care practice consisted mainly of physicians, with a few midlevel providers. At the time, "midlevel provider" was the term used to refer to physician assistants and nurse practitioners. These care providers were considered "less than" a real caregiver and, thus, unfortunately received the appellation "midlevel".

When I joined the group, I assumed the practice of an elderly physician who had just retired. He worked with a physician assistant named Jan, a gentle man who exuded kindness and compassion. Many patients referred to him as Dr. Jan and preferred him over any physician in the practice. I had never had the opportunity to work with physician assistants during my training, so I was initially unsure how to manage our interactions. However, that uncertainty quickly abated as we developed a lifelong professional and personal friendship.

It did not take me very long to realize that Dr. Jan could do almost everything I could do (and usually better). Although it was not the standard practice at the time, we began to share responsibility for a panel of patients. To the patients, we seemed almost interchangeable. It was a special working relationship that made me wonder why every primary care physician didn't work with a physician assistant. Such a relationship would enhance patient access and, if implemented correctly, improve the quality of care.

I want to make it clear that I am not taking credit for the genesis of a collaborative relationship between physician assistants and physicians. Furthermore, I was not the first to expand access by increasing the role of physician assistants or nurse practitioners. That said, in general in the early 1990s, the expansion of midlevel provider roles was not supported in the region where I practiced, and midlevel providers were not viewed as equals to physicians.

As I gained greater positional authority, first as Assistant Chief and then as Chief of Medicine, I decided to expand the roles of physician assistants and nurse practitioners. Physician-Physician Assistant dyads were created. Compensation was dramatically adjusted for Advanced Practice Clinicians (who were, by now, no longer called "midlevels"), and a new culture of teamwork and inclusivity was created. Whenever we hired a new physician, we ensured they were enthusiastic about working with advanced practice clinicians. If they had no interest in that type of working arrangement, we had no interest in including them in the organization.

Since the 1990s, the role of the Advanced Practice Provider (yes, the name has changed again) has evolved even more. In my area, more than 65% of primary care is delivered by physician assistants and nurse practitioners, and this share is expected to increase to 75% over the next 5 years. It is a remarkable transformation of the health care system.

Why am I sharing this story in a book about organizational structure? Because it is my best example of inclusivity. I am proud to live in an era where the discussion of diversity, equity, and inclusion (DEI) is commonplace. In the 1990s, those terms were rarely discussed; I am unsure if the phrase "DEI" was ever uttered. I am equally concerned that the current political administration is creating an environment in which these words once again feel taboo, and that we are taking a step back as a society.

As an organizational leader, I would ask you to consider creating a workplace that maximizes opportunities for diversity, equity, and inclusion. See if your workforce looks like, speaks like, and lives like the community you serve. If it doesn't, then take steps to fix it. Such small changes can have a massive impact on your organizational culture.

I would also ask you to take a broader view of the term's "diversity", "equity", and "inclusion". Often, leaders view this discussion as exclusively about race and gender (both of which are very important). I would urge you not to stop at the water's edge and expand your discussion to age, veteran status, homelessness, poverty, disability, and so many other factors. Even taking small steps in this direction creates an environment that distinguishes you from many other employers, improves society, and fosters a superior organization. My example of creating a level of training inclusivity environment for physician assistants and nurse practitioners may not have had the same impact as implementing more diverse hiring practices based on gender, ethnicity and other aspects of DEI. Still, there are very few wrong answers here, except the one in which you remain organizationally blind to the issue.

20

A Willingness to Change

"Things change at the speed of trust."

Doreen Fadus

Change in business is so common that change management has become its own industry. Books and courses explain how change should be done, and speakers will provide lectures on the topic. Change can be very stressful for an organization, but it is a necessary and inevitable part of every organization's cultural journey.

Our medical practice was large and had difficulties delivering a consistent quality of care across departments. We found that we could not improve outcomes by modifying our paper charts. At the same time, we were making an organizational transition from an ownership by an external entity to ownership by the providers themselves. We leveraged our previous owner's relationship with an EMR company, Epic Systems, to secure favorable pricing. Epic is now the largest vendor of EMRs worldwide and is widely recognized as the best EMR in the nation. However, at the time, it was a much smaller organization trying to build its reputation.

Many factors went into the decision to purchase an EMR. We considered price, productivity impact, and provider adoption as key factors. We also sought to determine whether we had the right culture to effect a change of this magnitude. After all the analysis, it came down to one essential question:

> *Are we, as leaders, willing to drive change in the face of uncertainty?*

The easy answer for many leaders is "yes". In fact, throughout my career, I have frequently answered "yes" to that question. If you have a large enough ego, you might answer that question with a "yes" every time. I would posit that there is a second question you should also ask:

> *Is there truly a greater purpose for the proposed change beyond financial gain?*

My editor will likely want me to remove the word "truly" from the last sentence, but in this case, I will resist. (Editor's Note: You can keep it. This time.) I use the word "truly" because most leaders can come up with another reason to justify a change beyond money, but if they are honest with themselves, they are only thinking about the money.

When implementing an EMR, our leadership was willing to make this change because we believed it would improve the quality of care that our patients received. It was this belief that allowed us to withstand the disaster that followed.

On October 31, 2005, I was sitting in a dark conference room at my medical practice in Chicopee. It was just after 7:00 a.m., and I was extremely nervous. Despite the date, my anxiety had nothing to do with Halloween. The walls were bare, and I sat in what we had optimistically labeled "the command center." The room was silent, and I remember hoping it would stay that way. It didn't.

This was the day we had been working toward for six long months: our transition from paper charts to an electronic medical record system. As the day unfolded, nearly everything that could go wrong did. Computers refused to power on, printers wouldn't connect, and the network crawled so slowly that even simple tasks felt impossible. Every complaint was funneled into the command center, where issues were scrawled onto oversized sheets of paper and taped to the walls. By the end of the day, those once-blank walls were completely covered—plastered with problems, frustrations, and evidence of unanticipated challenges. It was an unmitigated disaster. By any honest assessment, our change management efforts earned a solid "F."

You might remember my earlier chapter on "resilience". In retrospect, resilience enabled me to get through the six months that followed. It is easier to be resilient when you believe that the change you are making has a greater meaning and purpose. Over time, we resolved the implementation issues, and the EMR gradually became an integral part of our organizational success. It was also a reminder that, as an organization, we could identify and implement significant change.

Another example of change occurred when our leadership decided to create an anticoagulation clinic. Without getting too technical, there are several medical conditions which require patients to take blood thinners. At the time the only oral drug available for blood thinning was Coumadin which required the patients to monitor their progress through a blood test drawn in the laboratory. The result was sent to the ordering provider and then they decided to modify the dose of Coumadin accordingly. Unfortunately, with no established protocol on how to make medication adjustments, physicians used nonevidence based recommendations to guide their patients.

Fortunately, at the time, there was new technology that emerged that allowed patients to get a finger stick and use that information to adjust their Coumadin dose. In addition, there were studies suggesting that using this new technology in a protocol driven, nurse run clinic showed better outcomes for patients.

Given this information, the group leadership decided to do a pilot program to create an anticoagulation clinic and compare the results to that of our current process. The patients that were enrolled in the program came from physicians who would be considered "early adopters". The results were dramatic. Patients in the clinic were much better controlled than patients who were being managed through the provider driven process. The difference was so significant that leadership made the decision to unilaterally move all patients who needed Coumadin to be monitored through the clinic. The problem with this change was that no one, including myself, consulted the providers.

I had assumed that this would be one less task for the providers to manage. I thought they would be happy to transition this clinical function, but I could not have been more wrong. The providers were furious that we were considering this change. They felt strongly that they were best equipped to manage these patients and did not feel comfortable with potential liability issues. They felt so strongly that they refused to send their patients to the clinic.

I remember thinking if making this change was the "right thing to do"? In many cases, I felt a significant degree of uncertainty but not in this case. The outcomes were clear and the patient feedback was equally compelling. Patients much preferred a finger stick to a blood draw, and they loved the responsiveness of the nursing staff.

In retrospect, it was clear that there was a greater purpose to this change but there certainly was not a willingness from the providers. It took many one-on-one meetings to convince the providers that moving patients to the anticoagulation clinic was the clinically and ethically correct thing to do. Once they were convinced that were had a clinical motivation and were not chasing additional reimbursement, they bought into the change. Ultimately, the success of the clinic helped define the outstanding care of the medical group.

In both examples, there is one core, simple question: are you willing to assume responsibility for change as a leader, even when you know the road ahead will be bumpy? Find the courage and resilience to take this leap as long as it is underpinned with a genuine desire to "Do The Right Thing".

21

Leading Through Fear

"People don't follow titles, they follow courage. Leaders who lead through fear may command attention, but they never inspire loyalty."

John C. Maxwell

Have you ever worked for someone who seemed to lead through fear? Someone who relied heavily on positional authority, intimidation, or the implicit threat of consequences to influence the behavior of others? One might assume that this leadership style is uncommon and that organizations would readily identify and avoid placing such individuals in positions of authority. Unfortunately, both my personal experiences and years of interviewing prospective leaders suggest otherwise. Leaders who rely on fear and intimidation can be found across many industries and organizations.

Leadership driven by fear can take many forms. Some leaders are overt in their approach. They may raise their voices in meetings, use profanity, publicly criticize colleagues, or even threaten a person's job security. Others are far more subtle. They may establish unrealistic expectations around work hours, availability, or response times, creating an environment in which employees feel constant pressure to prove their commitment. While these expectations may never be stated as direct threats, they often carry an underlying message that failure to comply could have negative consequences.

When reflecting on my interactions with leaders who manage in this way, my initial reaction was often to view them as harsh, uncaring, or simply difficult people. Over time, however, I came to a different conclusion. Many of these individuals appear to struggle with their own insecurities. Lacking confidence in their ability to inspire through trust, collaboration, empathy, and mutual respect, they instead rely on authority and intimidation to achieve results. While this approach may generate short-term compliance, it rarely fosters the engagement, loyalty, and shared sense of purpose that characterize truly effective leadership.

Throughout my career I encountered many leaders who led through fear. Such leaders tend to be dominant personalities driven to achieve financial success. I am less interested in personality analysis, however, than in its effect on organizational culture. In my experience, leading through fear is actually very effective. As you may have read elsewhere or experienced yourself, fear is a powerful motivator. It should not be surprising, then, that it is equally effective in healthcare. Many employees seek clear direction, and dominant leaders often provide it. They follow up that decisiveness with a requirement that you follow their path, lest you be diminished within or terminated from the organization. Although I am certainly not a political scholar, I imagine this is not too different from authoritarian leaders around the world.

The question arises: Is appointing a CEO who leads through fear and decisive action a reasonable choice for an organizational leader? I would love to answer this question with a decisive "no", but I don't think it is that simple. The more appropriate answer is to ask another question: "What are you asking the CEO to do, and what is the current state of your organization?"

If you are in an organization that is failing and requires a rapid turnaround, having a decisive leader who instills fear may be a reasonable approach. I must admit that this approach runs counter to every fiber within my personal belief system. I do think, however, that you can make a cogent argument for this type of organizational culture and leadership in a particular circumstance.

However, leading out of fear is not sustainable. From a medical perspective, fear is an adaptive response. If you hear a wolf howling while you are out on a walk, you may immediately experience fear and a rush of adrenaline and run in the opposite direction. The human body can maintain this heightened state of fear for only so long. Prolonged fear often leads to feelings of anxiety and depression as well as multiple physical manifestations.

Fear, when used by a leader over an extended period, can cause significant organizational anxiety. Individuals who have job mobility leave the organization. Those who remain become emotionally numb; they come to work, do their job, and go home. They lose their connectivity to the organization and their sense of a greater purpose. When this starts, and it always does when a CEO leads with fear, it affects organizational outcomes. In medical environments, the quality-of-care decreases, patient experience scores drop, and employee engagement falters. It is at those times that boards of directors often reevaluate their leadership decisions and hire someone who brings a more kind, compassionate approach.

Could a balanced leader instill a measure of accountability and healthy respect while also demonstrating compassion and empathy? I am sure such leaders exist, but in my experience, they are relatively rare. The ideal leader would possess a balanced personality profile—someone who leads through persuasion rather than intimidation, inspires through example, and guides others with conviction, humility, and purpose. Equally important, they would have the ability to adapt their leadership style to the evolving needs of the organization and its people. Finding someone who embodies all these qualities is uncommon; that person would truly be a unicorn.

In assessing organizational culture and leadership, be honest about what you are seeking. Try to evaluate the situation your organization is currently experiencing - growth, turnaround, transformation etc. - and then try to match the characteristics of the leader to the situation in your organization. Hiring a leader who governs through fear may boost short-term financials, but within a few years, the culture will erode—forcing you to replace the CEO yet again.

22

Don't Forget to Breathe

"If you have done the best, you can - if you have done what you have to do - there is no use worrying about it.... You can't think about how it would be.... if you had done another thing. You have to decide."

Harry Truman

Serving as an effective leader is a stressful and challenging role. At times, you will make huge mistakes that can affect thousands of employees and clients. In addition, you will need to make decisions when there is no clear path and the "Right Thing To Do" remains elusive. You will seek input from your colleagues and friends, but despite their good intentions, their responses will not resonate with you. In some organizations, you may gain some solace in knowing that these decisions are not "life or death"; however, in healthcare, that is often not the case.

It is during these most private and difficult times that I have lost hours of sleep, become increasingly irritable with my family, and struggled with anxiety. I wish there was a simple formula that I could follow, but I haven't found one. It certainly is tempting to act quickly in the hope that, once a decision is made, you can move past these feelings of discomfort. Unfortunately, a rash decision rarely resolves a complex problem in the way you would like.

So, what should a leader do when they encounter this type of challenge? Whenever my executive administrative assistant and very close friend Barbara Schaler saw me feeling stressed, she would remind me to "just breathe". Her advice was simple but tremendously effective. I was always reminded of the need to be thoughtful and creative rather than to react impulsively. It reminded me to pause and reflect on any particularly difficult challenge.

I posit that everyone has a special place where they go to think about difficult things and that this place is rarely your office. For me, my go-to place is a warm shower. I used to think this was an unusual personal quirk, but it turns out there is a scientific principle that reinforces my observations. When you are in a warm, relaxing environment, your mind can wander, activating the brain's default mode for creative thinking and problem-solving. The lack of distraction and mild sensory deprivation caused by the steam and the water's white noise also contribute to the potential for increased insights.

Other leaders think best on the beach or on the golf course. The exact venue doesn't matter; finding your special place is a personal, invaluable resource for growth and well-being. It is ok to give yourself permission to walk away from endless meetings and take the time you need to consider deeply what is the right thing for you and your organization.

Once I take the time to reflect on the correct response to a challenging situation, the next step is to make the decision. It may seem obvious that, once you have settled on the "right" decision, you should just enact it. Unfortunately, CEO decisions often lead to significant organizational change, employee dissatisfaction, and occasional instability. I can comfortably say that no person, not even a CEO, enjoys making decisions that result in creating disgruntled employees.

In my leadership readings, I have come across two quotes that have truly impacted my approach to difficult decisions. As I noted in Chapter 14, Father Harry Cavanaugh, a former President of Notre Dame, described the characteristics his job required:

> *"Personal courage, often lonely courage, is essential for a great leader because everyone else below has passed the buck."*

The second quote is from President Harry Truman with which I chose to open this chapter. I must admit that I previously did not know much about President Truman except that he was the leader who decided to drop atomic bombs on Hiroshima and Nagasaki during WWII. When I saw the quote, it made me realize how incredibly challenging it must have been to decide to drop a nuclear bomb.

This is not a historical or political book, and I am certainly not making a statement about whether it was appropriate to use nuclear weapons in WWII. In addition, I am not comparing the decisions of the President of the United States with those of a Healthcare CEO. However, what resonates with me is that Harry Truman had to make one of the most difficult decisions imaginable. It's reasonable to assume he drew extensively on the expertise of subject matter specialists. Yet, in the solitude of the Oval Office, he ultimately bore the weight of a decision that would alter the course of history. Reflecting upon that decision, he noted the following:

"If you have done the best, you can - if you have done what you have to do - there is no use worrying about it.... You can't think about how it would be... if you had done another thing. You have to decide."

I really like Truman's emphasis on being thoughtful and informed, but at the end of the day, knowing that one must act: "You have to decide."

However, you should not allow one decision to define who you are as a leader. You are making the best decision you can with the information you have at a given moment. Sometimes, the outcome from your decisions will be awesome, and other times the results will be awful. As a physician, you make hundreds of these decisions every day. You must deal with the uncertainty of your decisions, and sometimes those decisions lead to a bad outcome. Sometimes your decisions lead to a patient experiencing adverse reactions, emotional distress, hospitalization, or even death. Yet inaction can lead to similar outcomes. You must decide.

Interestingly, my physician training taught me to never admit mistakes. The concern was that, if you were honest about your failures, you would be sued. In addition, the concept of apologizing to patients, openly admitting and addressing imperfection or, God forbid, failure, was beyond the pale. Fortunately, over time, these behaviors have changed, and it is now much more acceptable to admit failures and apologize to patients. In fact, patients tend to respect their doctor more when they are honest, and they are less likely to sue.

As an organizational leader, you must likewise learn to be humble, recognize that you are not perfect, and accept that you will make mistakes. You must acknowledge these errors, apologize for them, and move on. It is the combination of making difficult decisions thoughtfully, being accountable for the results, apologizing for mistakes, and showing resilience by continuing to make difficult decisions that constitutes the characteristics of a great leader.

Please take solace in knowing that nowhere in the above definition of a great leader was being "right" mentioned; it is much more about the courage to be wrong. As Teddy Roosevelt said, "You must dare to fail.

23

Leadership Mistakes: My Greatest Mistakes

"Leaders earn respect not by never failing, but by being willing to admit when they do, and to learn from it."

Frances Hesselbein

Mistakes and failure are part of being a leader, and it is essential that other leaders learn from "worst practices", so we don't repeat failures unnecessarily. In this chapter, I share some of my most significant mistakes in an attempt to help other leaders avoid common pitfalls.

Mistake #1: Premature Closure

It was a typical day in the outpatient office. I don't remember all the patient details from that day, but I probably saw a lot of hypertension, diabetes, high cholesterol, back pain, and depression. As the day drew to an end, I entered the exam room to see a middle-aged male with a chief complaint of fatigue. I must admit that the complaint of fatigue is so ubiquitous that it did not help me narrow the differential diagnosis. After we exchanged the standard greetings and I performed a full history and a focused exam, I sat down on the stool and shared with the patient that it was not clear to me exactly why he was fatigued. I would order some blood work, and we would get back together in a week to discuss the results and appropriate follow up.

For those of you not fluent in MD, a translation: I have no idea what's wrong with you and I hope to God the blood work gives me a hint. Perhaps an underactive thyroid or dehydration would neatly explain his symptoms and provide a simple treatment plan.

A couple of days later, I received the results of the patient's bloodwork. As I reviewed his results, I noted that his white blood cell count was markedly elevated and that his lymphocyte count (a type of white blood cell) was also significantly elevated. His blood work looked consistent with chronic lymphocytic leukemia (CLL), a serious illness that requires evaluation by a cancer specialist.

I immediately telephoned the patient and shared the results with him. I told him that his blood counts were reflective of CLL and that I was going to get him to see the cancer specialist as soon as possible. I described CLL to him and its implications. I also shared with him my rudimentary knowledge of prognosis and treatment. We spoke for around 30 minutes and, although I felt badly about the diagnosis, I felt good about our conversation.

About two weeks later, the patient saw the hematologist, a doctor who specializes in diseases of the blood. At the hematologists request thc patient had repeated the bloodwork prior to the consultation. At that visit, the hematologist reviewed the results which had returned to normal. This patient, whom I was convinced had a life-threatening illness, now had completely normal bloodwork. The patient did not have CLL. In fact, a viral illness likely caused the patient's fatigue and abnormal laboratory results. By the time the patient had repeated his blood work and seen the hematologist, his symptoms had resolved, and his blood counts had returned to normal. I felt like throwing up. I had been completely and totally wrong.

I knew the phone call was coming - it was inevitable. I wanted to ignore it but knew that was not possible. The patient started his conversation with me calmly but quickly escalated to yelling and screaming. He threw in several expletives and reminded me of my Hippocratic oath to "do no harm". He concluded with threats to sue me and suggested that I should consider another profession since I was clearly not competent to be a physician.

After finishing the conversation, I was emotionally drained. I felt horrible for making a mistake and putting the patient through an emotional rollercoaster through my incompetence. I tried to console myself by reminding myself that everyone makes mistakes and that no one is perfect. I also soothed my feelings by noting that my mistake did not cost anyone their life. None of these approaches provided me with any real solace. I just needed some time and distance but, unfortunately, healthcare doesn't give a lot of time for respite and reflection - I needed to see the next patient.

Over the 25 years since this patient interaction, I have reconsidered this mistake many times. Upon reflection, it all comes down to one thing: premature closure. I saw the patient, I assessed his physical findings, I reviewed the laboratory results, and I drew one and only one conclusion. Instead of allowing for a broader range of possibilities, I focused on one answer and excluded all others. It was probably a combination of arrogance and desire for expeditiousness that led me down this path.

What does this medical story about a poor decision have to do with being a good leader? Premature closure is one of the most common problems new and veteran leaders experience. The act of deciding without fully considering the range of possibilities is a pitfall that is avoidable, but it requires the leader's willingness to be humble and patient.

Here's another example. I had just been given the title of "Assistant Chief of Medicine". I was super excited to be in the role because it provided me both an increase in pay and some positional authority. Although my perspective on positional authority has evolved over time, at that stage in my career, I prioritized the value of having a formal title. I assumed it would engender respect among my colleagues, many of whom were much older and more experienced than I. In retrospect, it is clear to me now that a title just opens the door. If a leader is humble, hardworking, emotionally intelligent, and a collaborative decision maker, then they can walk through that door.

On this day, I was sitting in my office, completing notes between patients, when a medical assistant cautiously entered the room. She asked whether I was busy and whether I had a moment to discuss a situation she was experiencing with the physician with whom she worked. I invited her into my office, asked her to sit, and prompted her to tell her story. Although it happened long ago, I vividly recall the sense of importance I felt when I stepped into a position of authority and others began to seek my guidance to solve their challenges. It seems silly now, but power can be intoxicating in even its simplest forms.

This medical assistant spent the next fifteen minutes sharing her concerns. They revolved around the physician failing to respect her and routinely asking her to repeat blood pressure readings and recheck other key vital signs. She noted that he would then get upset at her because it took her too long and put him behind schedule. As she spoke, I absorbed every ounce of her anguish and distress. I felt her frustration and could not wait to talk to this unreasonable physician. I began to develop a storyline in which an arrogant physician used their positional power to demean a staff member. (In all fairness, this type of storyline is common in healthcare, so it was not a real stretch to apply it to this situation.)

After she completed her story, I thanked her for sharing her concerns with me and informed her that I would address them immediately. True to my word, I walked directly to the section of the building where this physician worked and asked the nurse to pull him out of the room. He reluctantly came out of the room and eyed me quizzically. I know he was assessing the situation, trying to remember who I was, and eventually recalling that I was the new Assistant Chief of Medicine. He then motioned me into his office. I took the opportunity to reintroduce myself with my new title and began to share the story of the unfairly treated medical assistant. I must admit, I was indignant as I shared the details.

After I completed my diatribe, I took a deep breath and refocused on the physician's face. To my surprise, it was not a face of contrition but rather a face of exasperation. He paused and asked me one question, "Have you spoken to the nursing supervisor about this medical assistant?"

At that moment, I felt a tremendous unease course across my body. It occurred to me that I had done nothing but take the medical assistant's words at face value. I had done no investigation at all. Driven by the urge to wield my new title and swiftly correct a wrong, I had rushed to judgment and plunged headlong into confrontation without fully thinking it through. This was a rookie mistake, which is so inviting that many leaders make it repeatedly over the course of their careers.

It turns out that this medical assistant had frequently been disciplined by her supervisor. She had on multiple occasions faked blood pressure readings and other vital signs to avoid falling behind or, more frequently, addressing her tardiness. As part of her remediation, she was required to repeat vital signs to ensure accuracy. Unsurprisingly, she did not share any of this with me when she raised her concerns.

If there are lessons to learn from my failures, it would come down to two points. The first would be to lead with humility. It is exciting to have a title, whether it is "Assistant Chief of Medicine" or "Chief Executive Officer". However, do not forget that it is only a title. Remain humble and never use your title to make a decision without getting adequate input. That level of arrogance can frequently lead to premature closure and bad outcomes.

Secondly, do your best to be patient. In my second example, I jumped quickly to a conclusion and completely bypassed any process that might have occurred. As a leader it is imperative to demonstrate patience and avoid jumping to conclusions. Acting impulsively often results in premature closure and rarely leads to the results you seek.

Mistake #2: Friends and Acquaintances

Around 2015, I was promoted to Medical Director. Like today, there was a significant physician shortage, and one of our clinical departments had been hit particularly hard by retirements and vacancies. Staffing levels had fallen well below what was needed to meet patient demand, and the remaining physicians were understandably focused on caring for patients. None had prior leadership experience or a strong interest in taking on administrative responsibilities. The situation posed a real challenge for the organization.

To help restore stability, I approached one of the physicians and asked whether he would be willing to serve as the department chief. He had never viewed himself as a leader, but he agreed to step into the role out of a deep sense of commitment to his colleagues and the organization. Over the following year, I watched him work tirelessly. He took on a demanding clinical schedule, covered for colleagues when needed, mentored less-experienced physicians, and somehow found time to manage the growing administrative responsibilities of the department. If that were not enough, he excelled at recruiting and played a key role in attracting new clinicians to the practice.

Twelve months later, the department had been transformed. Staffing levels had recovered, morale had improved, and operations were running smoothly once again. I felt relieved that an important part of the organization was thriving and grateful to have such a capable departmental leader in place. During that year, I had spent a great deal of time working alongside him, and we developed a close friendship. I use the word *friendship* intentionally. In earlier leadership roles, I had maintained a greater professional distance from those who reported to me, mindful of the responsibilities that come with supervision. In my new position, however, I placed greater value on collegiality and developed genuine friendships with several members of the leadership team. I respected them deeply, many having been recruited by me personally, and I had tremendous confidence in their abilities.

As the department became more stable, I began hearing occasional observations about the chief's leadership style. Initially, the comments were infrequent and nonspecific, but over time they became more consistent. Most centered-on communication, meeting dynamics, and interpersonal interactions—areas that often become more visible as a department grows and evolves.

When concerns about leadership effectiveness arose, I generally relied on a structured approach that emphasized open dialogue, clear expectations, and follow-up support. I tried to apply that process consistently across the organization. In this instance, however, I did not engage as quickly or directly as I might have under different circumstances. My admiration for—and friendship with—the department chief likely influenced my judgment. I believed strongly in his dedication and capabilities, and I hoped that the concerns would resolve naturally as the department continued to mature. Looking back, I recognize that earlier conversations would have been beneficial. Addressing concerns promptly would have been more consistent with the leadership principles I sought to uphold and would have better served both the individual and the organization.

Over time, I also came to appreciate that the leadership strengths that are invaluable during a period of crisis are not always the same strengths most needed in a period of stability. That insight, gained through experience, offered meaningful lessons for me as a leader. Here are two that may be helpful to others in similar roles:

1. As tempting as it may be to have your direct reports be your friends, do not cross that line. It is almost impossible to discipline a friend without jeopardizing both a personal and a professional relationship. On the contrary, if you don't discipline your friend when it is required in your job, you will not be fulfilling your organizational role, and others will question your integrity.
2. Just because someone is the right person for their job when they were hired does not mean they are still the right person a year or two later. Some leaders thrive in instability and chaos; others shine during transformation; and still others succeed only in situations of stability. When assessing your leadership team, consider their performance across various environments and determine whether they can adapt to the evolving work climate.

Mistake #3: Failure to Delegate

I will never forget one on-call night at the White River Junction Veterans Administration (VA) Hospital in 1991, even though it was about 35 years ago. I had just finished my internship and was now considered a resident.

The actual distinction between an intern in June and the second-year resident they become one month later is very small. Yet somehow, I was now a resident, and I was purportedly experienced and in charge. At the White River Junction VA in the evenings in 1991, there were only two physicians in the building, a resident and an intern. That night, I was the resident working with an intern named Susan. We oversaw the Emergency Room, the Intensive Care Unit, the Cardiac Intensive Care Unit, and all the patients on the floors. It was a daunting task, and everyone knew that this was when fledgling physicians became real doctors. Everyone also knew that no one working the shift would ever see a moment of sleep.

During the evening, I was called to the Intensive Care Unit (ICU) to evaluate a patient who was not doing well. It was clear that he needed additional monitoring and treatment, and the only way to do that was to put a catheter in his internal jugular vein, a big vein in the neck. By doing this, we could provide the patient with fluids and medication much more efficiently. The problem with this approach is that, right next to the big vein, lies a big artery, the carotid. If by mistake, I inserted the catheter into the carotid artery, very bad things could happen. By "very bad", I mean stroke, massive blood loss, and/or death. On the scale of badness, these rank pretty high.

It was very clear that this patient needed this procedure. Over the previous twelve months, I had performed this procedure more than five times, and I felt comfortable in doing it myself. I had taught only one other person to do it, and that experience went well, so I decided it was the right choice to let Susan gain the experience and place this IV. It also went along with the medical training credo, "See one, do one, teach one". It is probably a stupid credo, but in 1991, that was the common practice, so we obtained the appropriate consent and started the procedure.

I want to note that I made a conscious decision to delegate the procedure to the intern. I could have done it myself. I had the experience and was confident I could place it without difficulty. It would have been one more procedure to check off on my list of competencies. Why didn't I just do it? We will get back to that question later.

Susan meticulously placed a sterile drape around the patient. She used the carotid artery as a landmark and likely thought, "Vein good, artery bad." She carefully placed the needle into the patient's neck and saw the expected flash of blood. She was very excited and then gently slid a rubber catheter over the needle into what she thought was a vein. She then removed the needle. When you puncture a vein, it bleeds like a cut on your finger. When you put a hole in an artery, it shoots out like water from a fire hydrant.

I was standing behind Susan as she removed the needle. About three feet behind me was a white wall. Blood shot from the catheter, flew past Susan, hit the top of my right shoulder, and created a huge spatter on the wall behind us. There was a brief pause, much like the stunned silence after a child vomits on your shirt, followed by the sudden realization of what had just occurred. I looked at her and saw the absolute fear in her face. I wasn't feeling too great myself. I asked her what she thought we should do. She responded calmly but quickly. She said, "We should pull out the IV and apply pressure to the carotid artery."

With many medical decisions, there isn't always an obvious answer. Leaving the catheter in could have caused irritation of the artery and clotting. Removing the catheter could cause uncontrollable bleeding. Applying pressure to try to stop the bleeding could cause clotting of the carotid artery and a potential stroke or death. As I had been warned, the night shift at the VA turns students into physicians.

Susan pulled out the IV and applied pressure. We stood there in silence for a long time. We watched for signs of uncontrollable bleeding. We watched for signs of a stroke. In that moment, we forged an unspeakable bond that is impossible to describe. After enough time had passed, Susan removed her hand from the patient's neck. He was no longer bleeding, and he had not had a stroke. It was almost morning, so we decided to wait before determining our next steps.

I had chosen to delegate this procedure, and, at that moment, the outcome was bad. In fact, the outcome could have resulted in the death of a human being. In addition, when things were going poorly, I continued to delegate decision-making to see whether Susan knew what to do when the situation presented itself.

As an organizational leader, you may not be delegating in life-and-death situations, but you will certainly be able to meaningfully delegate meetings, projects, and decisions. You will have the opportunity to display trust in others by delegating. Good leaders delegate meaningful decisions; bad leaders don't.

I have often wondered why bad leaders don't delegate. Is it a lack of trust in other leaders, perhaps a lack of competence, or even a lack of work ethic? Although all of those may be contributing factors, I believe many bad leaders have huge egos and lack the humility to share the spotlight with others. They are less interested in building other leaders' confidence, less engaged in others' professional development, and more focused on their own accomplishments and accolades.

I have often heard about being a "servant leader". I honestly have no real idea what that means. What I do know is that, if you choose to be a humble leader, you can truly create an amazing organizational culture. As Lao-Tse said,

"There are 3 things in life which I hold fast and prize. The first is kindness, the second is frugality, and the third is humility. Be kind, and you can be bold. Be frugal, and you can be liberal. Be humble, and you can become a leader among men."

The patient did not have a stroke and eventually improved enough to be discharged from the hospital to a rehabilitation facility. Susan went on to become one of the best physicians in the entire residency program. She has since had an illustrious career and has taught others to be outstanding physicians, too. I like to think that, by giving her a chance to try, fail, and grow, I have played some small part in her successful career.

Mistake #4: A Line in the Sand

In this chapter, my mistake was not clarifying my personal limits early enough and remaining too long in a work environment that no longer felt sustainable for me.

As a new week began, I felt a growing sense of unease. Over the weekend, my supervisor had sent multiple messages about projects to complete, information to assemble, presentations to prepare, and difficult personnel decisions to consider. The pace and scope of the role left little separation between work and the rest of my life, and I struggled to establish meaningful boundaries.

Around that same time, my wife shared that I seemed distracted and emotionally unavailable at home. I was constantly checking my phone, and a single stressful message could derail my entire day. The persistent tension I carried began to affect both my personal well-being and my professional effectiveness. Others on the leadership team expressed similar discomfort, as the organization was moving quickly and priorities often shifted. The environment felt highly pressured, and decision-making was frequently urgent. Over time, this intensity took a toll.

That said, the purpose of this section is not to evaluate the qualities or effectiveness of any individual leader. Instead, it is about recognizing the moment when a direct report needs to step back and consider whether it is time to move on. Feeling conflicted in the face of a demanding supervisor is not uncommon. Senior leaders often weigh their responsibilities to their families, their teams, and the organization, and it is easy to justify staying longer than feels right.

So, when is it too much? When is it time to say no—to stop moving forward on a path that no longer aligns with your values? In the moment, those answers are rarely clear. Looking back, it is easy to see how often we rationalize, how readily we minimize our discomfort, and how long we delay action.

I did all those things. I remained in a role that increasingly challenged my sense of alignment and spent too much time trying to strike a balance between meeting expectations and preserving my own integrity. I knew I was approaching my personal limits. By the time I fully acknowledged that it was time to leave, I had already waited longer than I should have.

Late one night, unable to sleep, I finally confronted the question I had been avoiding: What is my line in the sand? I realized I already knew the answer. I also understood that staying much longer would likely require compromises I was no longer willing to make. Despite concerns about financial security, future opportunities, and leaving colleagues I respected, I made the decision to step away.

After notifying my supervisor, transitioning out of the role, and taking a brief sabbatical, I felt a profound sense of relief. The constant anxiety faded, and I gradually returned to a version of myself that my family and friends recognized. Several months later, I was able to find an organization that aligned with my values and organizational philosophy. I stayed in this job for the remainder of my career.

Most people have bosses, and few are immune to situations like this. My advice is simple: when you are not overwhelmed, take time to define your own line in the sand. That line will be different for everyone, shaped by personal relationships, financial realities, and individual values—but it exists for all of us. Write it down.

When you sense that you are approaching that line, pay attention. If raising concerns does not lead to meaningful change, it may be time to move on. Strong leaders and healthy organizations create environments where people are not asked to compromise their values in order to lead. If you find yourself feeling consistently misaligned with your role, stepping away may be the most responsible decision you can make.

Mistake #5: They Must Be Smarter Than Me

The most frequent question I receive is "Do you regret selling your medical group?" At the time of the sale, the group was a large, multispecialty private practice where I had worked for over two decades and served as CEO for several years. The answer to this simple question is complicated.

The group was doing well financially and had significant reserves. However, our forecast was not favorable. Our prognostications suggested that, despite our favorable situation at the time, we would run out of money within a year unless we made significant organizational changes.

As a result of our financial evaluation, we began investigating the sale of the practice. It seemed clear we could secure a significant sum by selling our practice while retaining some measure of autonomy. It appeared that selling would allow us to maintain our current organizational structure without layoffs.

As we discussed the options with the group, many of the physicians closer to retirement favored selling, while many of the younger physicians were more concerned about losing autonomy. At the time, I was the CEO, but I was also in the middle of my career; I was not a newbie, nor was I anywhere near retirement.

As the potential sale progressed, I started to have second thoughts. Would we really maintain autonomy? Couldn't we make the changes necessary without selling? Another voice in my head said, "They must be smarter than me." I believed that the more experienced physicians closer to retirement knew something I didn't. My doubts fell away, and I finalized the deal.

I wouldn't be telling this story if I didn't think I made a mistake. Several years after the deal closed, the medical group lost all autonomy. The group culture was destroyed, and there were extensive layoffs. Something I had spent my entire professional career creating disappeared in what felt like a heartbeat.

I am not the type of person who looks back very often. In fact, I frequently advise, "Make the best decision you can with the information you have at the time that you have it." Looking back is often filled with incomplete scenarios where you make endless assumptions about how things might have turned out if you had made a different decision. The truth is that you often have no idea how the universe would have unfolded if you had chosen a different path.

That said, I regret selling the medical group I led, but perhaps not for the reason you think. It is easy to regret the decision, knowing now that the group lost its autonomy and can no longer boast of being one of the most creative and highest-quality groups in Massachusetts. It would be easy to regret the fact that, despite promises from the acquiring entity, many physicians and staff lost their jobs.

The actual reason I regret selling the medical group is that I allowed others' influence to sway me to the point where I doubted my own judgment. As the CEO, you always want input, but for these types of organizational decisions, the final call is yours. There is a considerable difference between input and influence. In one of the most important decisions of my career, I allowed input and self-interest to spill over into influence, and I still second-guess that decision.

You will always have smart people providing you with suggestions. It is your job to ensure their suggestions serve the organization, not their own or your own interests. Try your best to be collaborative, but make sure to put the organization's needs first, and don't shy away from hard things. In my case, refusing to sell and making the changes necessary for success would have been incredibly difficult. What I learned is that by selling, or shying away from the difficult decisions, I did not avoid them. I just delayed them until someone else stepped in and did the things that I should have done in the first place.

Mistake #6: Texting and Email Are So Convenient

I was looking at my phone the other day and reviewing what applications I use the most. Unsurprisingly, email and texting dominated my usage. I am old enough to recall what it was like before this form of communication, and I want to be the first to say that it is so much better now.

When I think about my professional life and how much time I have spent communicating through email and text, it is hard to believe that anything got done before these technologies. Despite my frequent use of email/text, I am a strong believer in personal interaction. During the pandemic, the delivery of healthcare changed dramatically. Visits for many types of medical problems became virtual, and there was a belief, which some still hold, that health care would never be the same. As the pandemic receded, organizations have formed to provide only virtual care, promising convenience and quality. When you add artificial intelligence to the equation, it can seem inevitable that the future of health care will involve minimal human interaction.

Interestingly and perhaps counterintuitively we are starting to see that human interaction remains an essential part of health care. Patients want in-person visits and hands-on exams. Virtual visits have decreased to about 15% of all patient visits according to a 2026 article in the journal "Healthcare." The need for personal interaction seems innate to human beings and essential to their healthcare experience.

I remember a visit from a young woman who came in with headaches. As I was taking a standard history, it became clear that she was very uncomfortable. She was fidgeting in her chair and would not make eye contact with me. She picked at her nails and spoke in a very soft voice. It is hard to describe, but I knew from her nonverbal cues that something was not right. After asking some additional questions, I asked her if she had ever been hit or abused by a family member or partner.

The anxiety in the room was palpable. Her body tightened, and she stopped picking her nails, trying to garner the courage to answer the question. The mood was heavy, but I could feel a connection building between us. I knew that if I could just wait and listen, there would be safety in that moment, allowing her to share a deep secret. She ultimately looked up at me and, through her tears, shared that she was being physically abused by her husband, who was just outside in the waiting room. She lifted her shirt and showed me the bruises all over her chest and abdomen.

For the remainder of the visit, I provided her with information and support. I tried to convince her that she should consider going to a domestic abuse shelter and leave her abusive situation. Unfortunately, she felt trapped and did not feel ready to leave.

I share this story because I feel very confident that, if this interaction had occurred over a virtual visit, I would have had a very difficult time noting her nonverbal cues. I certainly would not have noticed her fidgeting, nail picking, and inability to maintain eye contact. Even with video, it would have been very challenging to pick up on these cues.

It has occurred to me that leading an organization through emails, text, and videoconferencing risks similar pitfalls to remote patient visits. The subtlety of human interaction is lost. Conveying hope, compassion, trust, and emotion can be done remotely, but something is lost in the translation.

So, what mistake is being made? It's one I make every day. I choose the convenience of technology over the intimacy of human interaction. Every day, I chose to email a colleague who may be just down the hall. Every day, I choose to send out group emails or organizational announcements instead of calling in-person all-staff meetings or making departmental visits.

I am not asking for the genie to be put back in the bottle. Technology is here to stay, and we should embrace it. However, if you are going to build a strong organizational culture, you need to step away from your computer, walk down the hall, and make an in-person connection. You would be amazed at the impact a personal visit to staff can have on your success as a leader. If you combine that with a true interest in their thoughts and ideas, you are more than halfway to a great organization.

Mistake #7: Accountability Versus Fear

The mantra of every new leader arriving at an organization that is experiencing challenges is something along these lines:

"I have come to listen and better understand the organization. Once I have done that, I want to make sure we have clear expectations and create a meaningful sense of accountability". On the surface, this leadership strategy makes sense. We all want a leader who is a good listener. We all want a leader who is clear with their expectations. We all want a leader who holds people accountable (As long as it's not us, they are talking about). If you can find a leader who does all these things while remaining kind, considerate, and humble, you really have something.

I have met many leaders who confuse driving accountability with creating fear. Those who cross that fine line struggle to create the organizational culture I am outlining in this book. When accountability becomes fear, the work culture allows for no psychological safety, so good people quit. Said more directly, when your leader is a jerk, coming to work sucks, and no one wants to stay!

I have so many examples of leaders creating fear in their employees. I imagine that, if you are reading this book, you have plenty of examples as well. One of the more egregious situations I experienced was in medical school. During a rotation in vascular surgery, I was holding a retractor, an instrument used to hold back tissues or incision edges, so the surgeon has a clear view and access to the operative field, during a very complicated vascular bypass procedure of the lower extremity. These surgeries typically lasted 4-6 hours, and as a student, your role was typically limited to observing or holding retractors. After about 4 hours, as the surgery was nearing completion, the surgeon handed me surgical scissors and asked me to cut the remaining suture above the surgical knot that he had tied. He knew that I had poor depth perception due to blindness in one eye, but he did not care. I began to reach into the surgical field so I could grab the sutures and cut below my fingers but above the knot; it was the only way I could accomplish this task, given my disability. The surgeon then slapped my hands away and threw a scalpel at me. He shouted, "Never touch my sutures! Get out of my operating room!"

I left the room, feeling relieved that the scalpel did not hit me and that I could sit down after four hours. I had quickly learned a lesson about how this surgeon liked his knots cut. I would never make that mistake again. I also feared him, avoided him and never pursued any surgical experiences again.

It would have been fine for the vascular surgeon to share with me how he wanted his sutures trimmed. It could have been a great teaching moment, and I would have been accountable for that in the future. Unfortunately, the surgeon chose intimidation and fear. While this may have been his desired effect in the short term, his behavior created many unintended ripples.

Intimidation takes many forms in healthcare and leadership. Sometimes, it is as blatant as throwing a scalpel or publicly disparaging your direct reports, but other times it is more subtle. In some ways, subtle intimidation is more devastating to an organization because it is harder to prove and more difficult to weed out. Some leaders who keep individuals accountable to their tasks quickly raise the bar to a point that failure is inevitable. Leaders like this are unpredictable and create a sense of angst in the organization.

So here is my advice: create standards and hold people accountable, but be predictable, transparent, kind, and humble. Most employees understand that difficult decisions need to be made in organizations. They may not like the outcomes of your decisions, but your culture will survive if you follow a predictable process and make decisions that are for the greater good of the company. However, if you drive a culture of unpredictability and fear, the outcome really doesn't matter; the organization will ultimately fail because fear is a short-term motivator.

24

Teach Them How to Say Goodbye

"The measure of a statesman is not how long he holds office, but how gracefully he relinquishes power."

Henry Kissinger

I love history, theater, and music. It should be no surprise, then, that seeing "Hamilton" on Broadway and then once again on tour in Connecticut was an experience I will never forget. If you have not had the opportunity to see this musical performance, I would encourage you to find the time and resources to experience this brilliant depiction of the life of Alexander Hamilton.

I will not retell the story here, but I do want to share one specific scene that touches my heart and has a significant relationship to organizational culture. George Washington served two terms as the first President of the United States. He was an extremely popular general and could almost certainly have been elected to a third presidential term. Still, he made a decision that would change the course of American history forever. He voluntarily stepped down from the most powerful position in the nation. George Washington believed he had served his country and that it was time to establish a precedent for a peaceful transition of power. In a life of extraordinary accomplishments, you could argue this was one of his most significant and most selfless acts.

In the play, the song "One Last Time" describes a conversation between Alexander Hamilton and George Washington about this decision. Beyond its beauty, the song emphasizes the importance of an organization not being overly dependent on a single individual but rather developing a process that will outlive any one person. It also focuses on the importance of learning how to say goodbye. This concept of creating an organization or, in the case of George Washington, a nation that can survive and prosper after its current leader steps down, is the final piece of building organizational culture.

When a leader joins an organization, one of the first and most vital steps is to get to know the group and its current culture. The prevailing view is that this listening phase takes approximately three months. In fact, there is a very popular leadership book by Michael D. Watkins titled The First 90 Days. This book describes how a leader might transition into their new role and make key decisions in their first three months. It is an excellent book and provides a roadmap that can be very helpful for new leaders. That said, 90 days is not a very long period.

Most leaders arrive with their own agenda. They go through their first 90 days on a listening tour, but for the most part, they already know what they want to do and how they want to do it. They want to get going, produce early wins, and develop a new organizational culture. Although I certainly understand this approach, I believe it is misguided.

When considering a new leader, it is essential to take the time to understand the existing culture and the leadership team before implementing key changes. It is so common for new leaders to bring in their own teams and ignore the talent in front of them. It is also easy to misjudge talent within an organization when you make rapid leadership changes. As a mentor of mine says, "Let it breathe. Have the courage to be patient and do nothing".

After you've made your initial connections within your organization, you'll likely enter what I call your "internal phase". This is simply a recognition that you don't yet know the existing culture well and need time to learn it. In large organizations, this often takes a while. This internal focus is essential for understanding the nuances of your organization—learning who the key people are and beginning to make meaningful process changes that will drive success.

In my experience, your internal phase typically lasts around three years. Identifying problems, implementing change, and measuring results all take time. This period also allows you to build deep connections with your team and the organization. Resist the temptation to focus your energy externally unless the situation absolutely requires it. External distractions during your formative years as a leader can create a sense of disconnect from your team. If you can develop trust, it becomes much easier for your team to carry forward your vision even when you're not in the room.

Most recently, I worked with a team I have known for over a decade. The job required me to spend a great deal of time outside of the office. My role required traveling to physician offices and delivering a series of presentations to the community. During that period, I delegated most organizational decisions to the senior leadership team. When I asked them how things were going, the most common responses I received was, "We did what you would have done in this situation" or "we tried very hard to do the right thing." Culture like this requires time and presence to create, but once it is there, it can survive without you.

After three years in a CEO role, it is typically time for a leader to transition from an internal focus to a greater external focus or community presence. Your job is not to be a Chief Operating Officer. Your job is to set direction and connect with your membership and clients. Depending on your personality type, this transition is either a relief (for those who don't like the detailed nature of operations) or a disaster (for those who are introverted and always wanted to be a COO). Either way, it is a natural progression of leadership. You will be well-positioned to interact with the external aspects of your job with a strong foundation and understanding of your organization.

After six years, a leader typically begins to reflect. Every situation is different and there is tremendous value to experience, but, by six years, you have had enough time to instill a culture that should be able to survive your departure. If you have taken the typical leadership path, you have started to lose connection to the organizational operations, and many of your key strategic plans have already taken flight. You should start considering a transition.

Somewhere between your sixth and ninth years as an organization's CEO, you should be asking yourself, "If I say goodbye, can the organization learn to move on? Can it outlive me?" The answer to this question is almost certainly "yes", but you should consider what you have done to prepare the organization for future success. If you only begin asking this question in the seventh year of your tenure, the likely answer is that you have not done enough. The other key question is whether you have the humility to move on.

In an earlier chapter, we discussed the importance of humility in a leader. This is typically something we consider when we hire someone. We consider if they work well with others and if they can share the credit of successes while owning failures on their own. Rarely do we ask whether a leader has enough humility to walk away when it is time.

Many CEOs have a large ego. In some ways, this characteristic is essential for making the difficult decisions that affect large populations of employees and their families. However, when the time is right, can this leader suppress their ego and step away?

In 1797, after eight years as the first President of the United States, George Washington walked away. There were no rules requiring him to step down as President. Instead, he identified a greater purpose for his role and the humility to execute it. In his farewell address, he said:

> *I shall carry with me the hope that my country will never cease to view... [my errors] with indulgence and that, after forty-five years of my life dedicated to its service with an upright zeal, the faults of incompetent abilities will be consigned to oblivion, as myself must soon be to the mansions of rest.*

Washington demonstrated tremendous humility in asking his countrymen to forgive his failures, showed unprecedented foresight and courage in prioritizing a peaceful transfer of power over personal ego and ambition, and set a timeless example of leadership grounded in principle rather than self-interest. For the sake of your organization and the culture you have developed, don't overstay your welcome. Instead, take inspiration from George Washington and be proactive even in your departure.

25

Some Parting Advice

As I began writing this book, I was preparing to retire from healthcare after over 30 years. As part of the transition process, I prepared a document that included key meetings, key contacts, active issues, a month-by-month calendar of key activities, and, finally, some thoughts and advice. As I was composing the advice section of the transition document, it occurred to me that it would be a helpful, concise list of key takeaways for my book on organizational culture. I have made a few modifications to the actual document, but it has maintained the key elements, which I believe could be very helpful to new leaders anywhere.

Essential:

1. Just be you: You are an amazing leader with tremendous personal strength. Don't try to be someone else. Find strength in knowing that any successes or failures come not from trying to emulate someone else but because you are following your own path.

2. Remember your title: You are the CEO: You are not the COO, CHRO, CIO, or CFO. It will take a while, but you will need to learn how to be involved in operations, finance, IT, and HR and yet not run them. It is tempting to continue to focus on things that you are good at (and often enjoy), but that is no longer your role.
3. Patience: This job requires patience. It is rare that a quick response is needed or appropriate even though everyone else wants you to respond quickly and decisively. Breathe. Get multiple opinions and then do what you think is right.
4. Be an Architect and an Arsonist: In creating your own path, it is important that you change or eliminate aspects of the organization that don't mesh with your vision. In fact, it is essential to thoughtfully and strategically burn down parts of the previous infrastructure to make room for new paths. Don't be held back by previous dogma or what others will think. Your job is to be an architect for the future, applying new ideas that will build long-term organizational resilience. Respect and honor the past but, at some point, leave it there and embrace the future.
5. Remember to forgive: Most of your employees are trying their best to do the right thing, but they are going to make mistakes. You can take a hard line, or you can forgive them. Choose forgiveness, and you will be surprised by its impact on your culture.
6. Remember to delegate. Physicians are notorious for believing that they can do everyone's job better than the person doing it. That is not an effective leadership style. Take the risk and delegate with oversight. You can't do it all yourself.
7. Not everything is an emergency: Don't make your lack of planning an emergency for everyone else. Don't call

unplanned meetings and pull everyone away from their important work. Doing so makes you appear unfocused and unappreciative of the time of others.

Important

1. Learn how to say "No": As a leader your time and presence will always be requested. It is tempting to say "yes" and try to meet everyone's needs. Unfortunately, not only is this not feasible from a time perspective, but it also inhibits the growth of other leaders who need to learn to make important decisions without you in the room. If you struggle with saying "no", make sure you develop a support structure that can help you set boundaries or occasionally run interference for you.
2. Confrontation: Confrontation is always draining and is very hard to leave at work. Take solace in knowing that your role is to "Do the Right Thing" for the organization and not necessarily every individual. As Spock from "Star Trek" would say, "The needs of the many outweigh the needs of the few".
3. Don't hold on to a problem: When you know that an employee is not right for the organization, try to move them on as quickly as possible. This is better for the organization, but even more importantly, it is better for that individual.
4. Be present: The real work doesn't happen behind your desk. You don't need to be in an episode of "Undercover Boss", but you do need to get out of your office and interact with your employees (and not just your senior leadership team). It is not enough to show a PowerPoint at the All-Staff Meeting or just walk through an office and wave. Sit with the frontline employees, eat lunch with them, and try to get to know

at least some of them as people. It will make you a better leader, but, more importantly, it allows your employees to know you as a person, not just a title.

5. Be accountable: Here is a mantra every CEO should consider (at least publicly): All the organization's successes are the result of the hard work and expertise of my employees. All the organization's failures are the result of my inability to build the culture necessary for organizational success.
6. Positional Authority: Don't use your positional authority to demean others. I know I said this earlier in the book, but it really upsets me, so I had to repeat it here.

Considerations

1. Keep one thing: Make sure to hold on to one thing that brings you joy. For me, that has always been teaching. Find that thing for yourself and don't give it up.
2. Set short- and long-term goals: At the beginning of each year, set goals for yourself. If you don't set these milestones, you will find yourself being forever reactive.
3. Create a legacy: Create something you can look back upon that makes you feel like you have made a difference. Before you begin the job, think about what you want yours to be and write it down.
4. Balance: At the end of the day, it is just a job. You will make acquaintances and have tremendous memories, but, when it is over, you will be left with your family and friends. Don't wait till you are done with your career to have fun. Take 30 minutes each month to reevaluate your boundaries. Get out of meetings you don't need to be at, create time in your schedule

to relax and think, work from home when you need to, and, occasionally, take an afternoon just for yourself.

5. Senior Leadership Team: You will be inheriting a leadership team. Make sure the team members fit your needs and leadership style. Don't be reluctant to make changes when needed.
6. Phone a Friend: Don't be stubborn and spend hours on an issue when a quick call would address your concerns.
7. Executive Coach: Consider finding an executive coach and building support for this relationship into your contract. It is lonely managing the political landscape. An objective ear is always helpful.
8. Transition Effectively into Your New Role: Read "The First 90 Days" by Michael Watkins.
9. Send Later: When you have a great idea that you want to share with your team, but it is Saturday night, use the "Send Later" function for text and email.
10. New staff orientations: If you really want to change the culture, you need to set the expectations from the first day. If you can convey your vision to new employees and they can connect with you as the CEO, then you have already gone a long way to creating culture. In addition, new employees bring fresh ideas and eyes to your teams and processes.
11. New perspectives. I will never forget interviewing a candidate for an administrative assistant position. I greeted her at the entrance and led her down a long hallway toward my office. Unfortunately, I ignored a piece of advice my wife had often given me: when walking with someone, walk beside them, not ahead of them. As a result, I found myself several steps in front of the candidate as we made our way down the corridor.

When I reached my office door and turned around, I noticed that she had stopped to straighten a picture hanging on the wall. I remember thinking that I had walked past that same picture hundreds—perhaps thousands—of times without ever noticing that it was crooked. For a moment, I felt a little embarrassed. Then I realized I had just been given an important reminder: fresh eyes see things that familiarity often overlooks.

It was a simple act, but it reinforced a lesson that has stayed with me throughout my leadership career. New people bring new perspectives, and those perspectives can reveal opportunities, problems, and possibilities that those of us who have been around for years may no longer see.

Authors Notes

Update:

In the "In Memoriam" section of this book, I wrote about my mother. Notably, I shared the following, "I looked out to my right and saw four deer standing in our yard. Deer in Connecticut are not unusual but in the several years we had been there we had never seen one in our yard. When I opened the door two of the deer quickly scattered but two of them remained. I called my wife to come to the door and by the time she got there only one was left. It was no more than 10 to 15 yards away, staring directly at me.

I am not a religious man. I like to think of myself as a man of science after all my years in medicine. I do not believe in reincarnation, and I am not sure I believe in life after death. I also know for certain that, just for a moment, I saw my mother in that deer. She was there to say goodbye and to let me know that she was still there. That she still believed in me."

In the time that it has taken to write this book, my father became ill and passed away. At the time of his death, my dad was staying in assisted living and my brother, Brian, and I were visiting but staying a couple of miles away. We received the call of his passing at around 3:00 in the morning. Instead of waiting till sun break, we decided to drive down immediately to the assisted living facility. As we drove out of our driveway and down the street, we had to stop abruptly. In the middle of the street, staring directly at us was a deer. It paused and looked at us momentarily and then gradually finished crossing the street.

I can't emphasize enough that I am a man of science, but it is very difficult to reconcile that twice in my lifetime, moments after my parents had passed, that I had chance encounters with deer. It certainly could be just a random circumstance, but I can't help but think it could be something more.

Appreciation

I never thought I would enjoy writing a book. The concept always seemed so overwhelming, and I just wasn't sure that I had anything meaningful to say. It turns out I loved the process of writing and found tremendous joy in sharing thoughts and insights from my life experiences. As I bring this book to an end, I feel the need to thank my family for their encouragement and support. My wife, Elie, provided me with the time, space and love to bring this book to fruition. My son, Thomas, served as the impetus and first editor for this project and always had an encouraging comment which propelled me forward. Finally, my daughter Rachel, who recently received her master's in public health from Boston University, always provided me with emotional support and positive feedback. Her support made me feel like writing this book might touch someone and make a difference.

The list of contributors to this book is long, and many of them don't even know they played an important role in my journey. Below is an attempt to recognize those who have touched and continue to touch my life:

High School:
Pierre Latour

College:
Mark Lagon, Dave LeLacheur, Maura Padula, Rod Harten

Medical School:
Tom Cataldo, MD

Residency:
Scott Donaldson, MD

Siblings:
Brian Shuman, DMD, Lou Shuman, DMD, Jody Shuman

Colleagues:
Barbara Schaler, Brian Banker, MD, Carlos Martins, Dan Weiswasser, MD, Tom Yu, MD, Gina Ohanesian, MSOB, Donna Hanifan, Denise Adamczyk, RN, Amy Roy, RN, Karen Stefanik, RN, Julianne Dias, RN, Devon Melao, RN, Michael McDonald, PA, Kathy Orcutt, Tim Fallon, Jason Carvalho, Ann Shain, MD, Kristin Morales-Lemieux, Vanessa Smith, Mark Keroack, MD, Jan Szewczynski, PA, Dwayne Long, Scott Markham, Psy.D., Kristin Woods, MD

Friends:
Ted and Cindy McCarthy, Tom and Carolyn Gernux, Bob and Terri Maggi, Ben and Joyce Smar, Andy and Hutt Beall, Alex Lin, MD, Suzy Takacs NP

References

Chapter 2:

AID Feedback Model: Action–Impact–Desired outcome feedback framework. Unpublished leadership development model commonly used in healthcare and organizational leadership training.

Chapter 4:

Lencioni, P. (2025). Hiring ideal team players: An interview guide to help you identify candidates who are humble, hungry, and smart. The Table Group. https://www.tablegroup.com/topics-and-resources/managing-people/ideal-team-player-hiring-guide

Chapter 6:

Khurshid, M. (2023, October 14). Have we ever thought about this? Medium. https://mohsinkhurshid.medium.com/have-we-ever-thought-about-this-903df5d5b9b1

Chapter 7

Unknown. (n.d.). If you are not trying and failing, you are not trying hard enough.

Goodwin, D. K. (2018). Leadership: In turbulent times. Simon & Schuster.

Woodruff, J. (Interviewer), & Goodwin, D. K. (2018, October 9). Doris Kearns Goodwin on what today's leaders can learn from past "turbulent times" [Interview]. PBS NewsHour. https://www.pbs.org/newshour/show/doris-kearns-goodwin-on-what-todays-leaders-can-learn-from-past-turbulent-times PBS

Chapter 8

Sherman, R. M., & Sherman, R. B. (1977). The wonderful thing about Tiggers [Song]. On The many adventures of Winnie the Pooh [Soundtrack]. Walt Disney Records.

Chapter 9

Phillips, D. J. P. (2014, April 14). How to avoid death by PowerPoint [Video]. TEDxStockholmSalon. YouTube. https://www.youtube.com/watch?v=Iwpi1Lm6dFo

Chapter 10

Cadigan, S. (n.d.). Acquisition, retention, engagement [Talent strategy keynote overview]. Cadigan Talent Ventures. Retrieved December 17, 2025, from https://stevecadigan.com/topics/acquisition-retention-engagement

Kim, J., Bailey, E. V., Hayworth, S., Illapperuma-Wood, C., Weir, R., Fischer, A., & Weir, P. (2026). National trends in telehealth utilization, 2020–2023: Post-pandemic trends from the Medical Expenditure Panel Survey. *Healthcare*, *14*(3), 331. Furihata, R. (Ed.).

Chapter 12

Keller, G. W., & Papasan, J. (2013). The One Thing: The Surprisingly Simple Truth Behind Extraordinary Results. Bard Press.

Chapter 15

Doogie Howser, M.D. (1989–1993). Created by S. Bochco & D. E. Kelley. ABC Television.

Chapter 17

Undercover Boss. Created by Stephen Lambert, executive producers Stephen Lambert, Jack Burgess, Mike Cotton, and Rachel Bloomfield, CBS, 7 Feb. 2010–present. Reality television series.

Chapter 18

Covey, S. R. (1989). The 7 Habits of Highly Effective People. Free Press.

Chapter 24

Miranda, Lin-Manuel. Hamilton: An American Musical. Hamilton: The Revolution, edited by Jeremy McCarter, Grand Central Publishing, 2016.

Watkins, M. D. (2013). The First 90 Days: Proven Strategies for Getting Up to Speed Faster and Smarter (Updated and expanded edition). Harvard Business Review Press.